ENCHANTING REVERSE COLORING BOOK

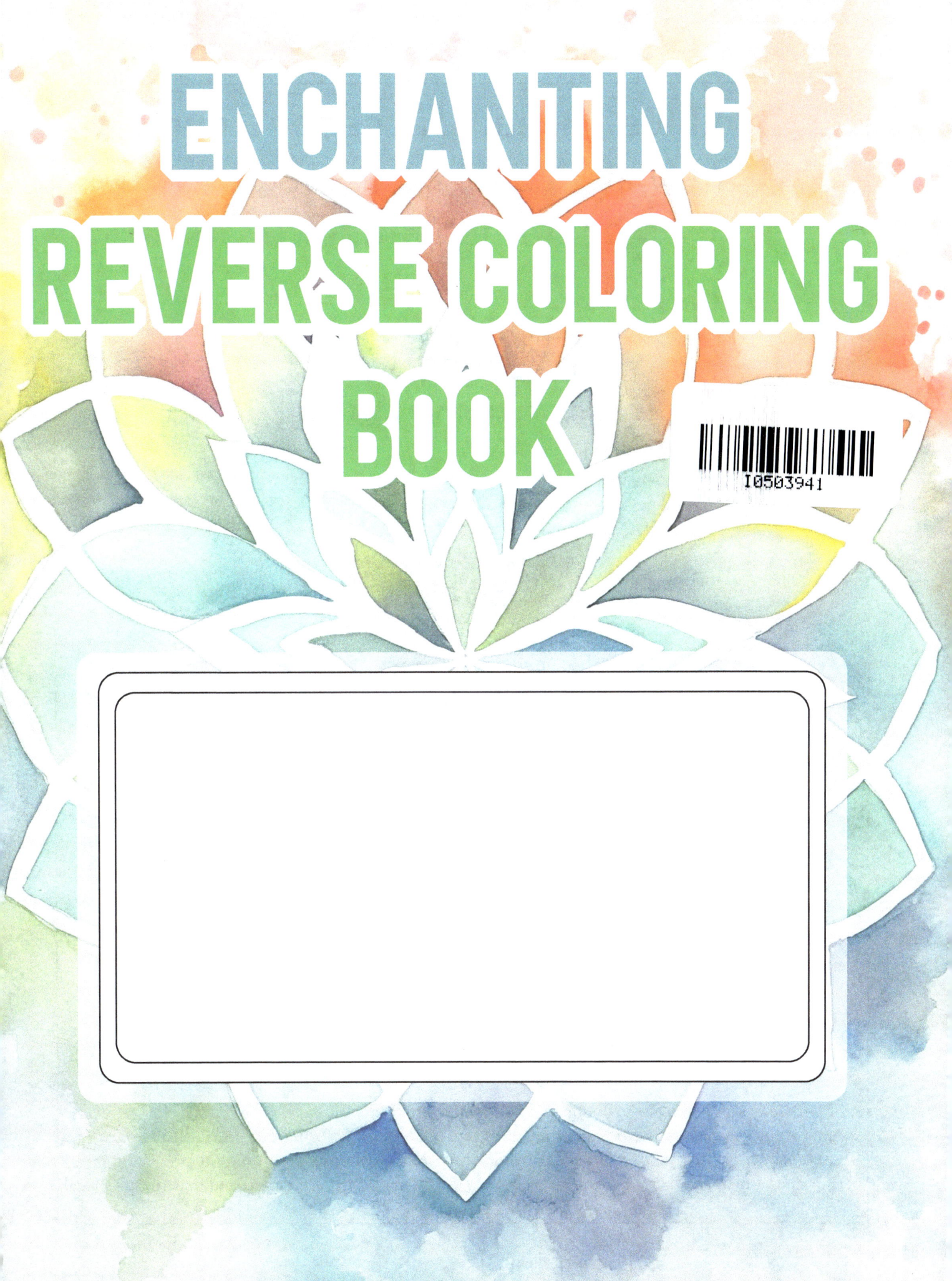

Join us for early access to our new releases, bonuses and recommendations.

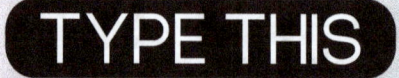

bit.ly/celeste_nightshade

OR

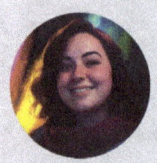

COPYRIGHT © CELESTE NIGHTSHADE

YOUR HONEST OPINION
IS VALUABLE FOR US

PLEASE LEAVE A
REVIEW FOR THIS BOOK

HOW TO USE THIS BOOK

MATERIALS NEEDED:

'Reverse coloring book' And Pencil or pen only.

EXPLORE THE PAGES:

Open the book to any page and observe the abstract watercolor design.
Let your imagination run wild as you try to identify shapes or objects within the design.

CREATE LINE ART:

- Use a pencil or pen to lightly sketch lines based on the shapes you see.
- Be creative and experiment with different lines, curves, and angles to bring your vision to life.
- Feel free to blend colors, add details, or make adjustments to enhance your artwork.
- Once finished, share your creations with friends, family, or on social media to inspire others.

EMBRACE THE JOURNEY:

Remember, the reverse coloring book is about embracing your imagination and creating unique artworks. Don't worry about making mistakes; enjoy the process and let your creativity flow freely.

REPEAT AND EXPLORE:

Keep exploring different pages and designs in the reverse coloring book. Experiment with different techniques, colors, and ideas to continuously challenge and inspire
yourself.

MENTAL HEALTH BENEFITS OF USING REVERSE COLORING BOOKS:

Stress Relief : Making lines and painting in the reverse coloring book reduces stress and promotes relaxation by focusing on the present moment.

Mindfulness : Immersing in the book's creative process fosters a state of flow, bringing mental clarity and inspiring new ideas.

Self-Expression : Creating line art allows freedom to visually express emotions, thoughts, and experiences, boosting self-esteem.

Cognitive Stimulation: Engaging in the book stimulates problem-solving and visual-spatial skills, enhancing cognitive functioning.

Positive Mood and Well-being: Creating art uplifts mood, increases self-awareness, and provides a sense of accomplishment, enhancing overall well-being.

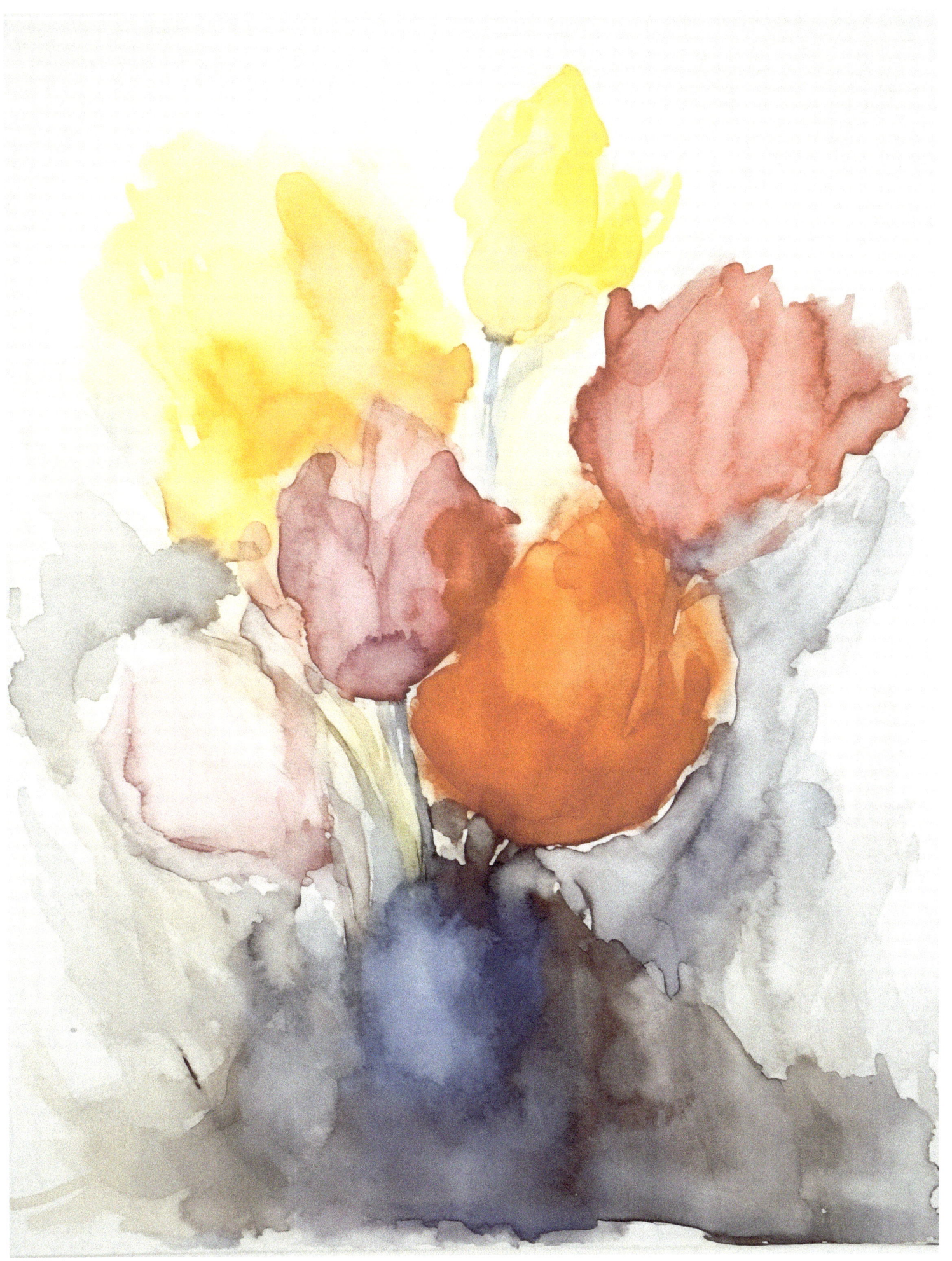

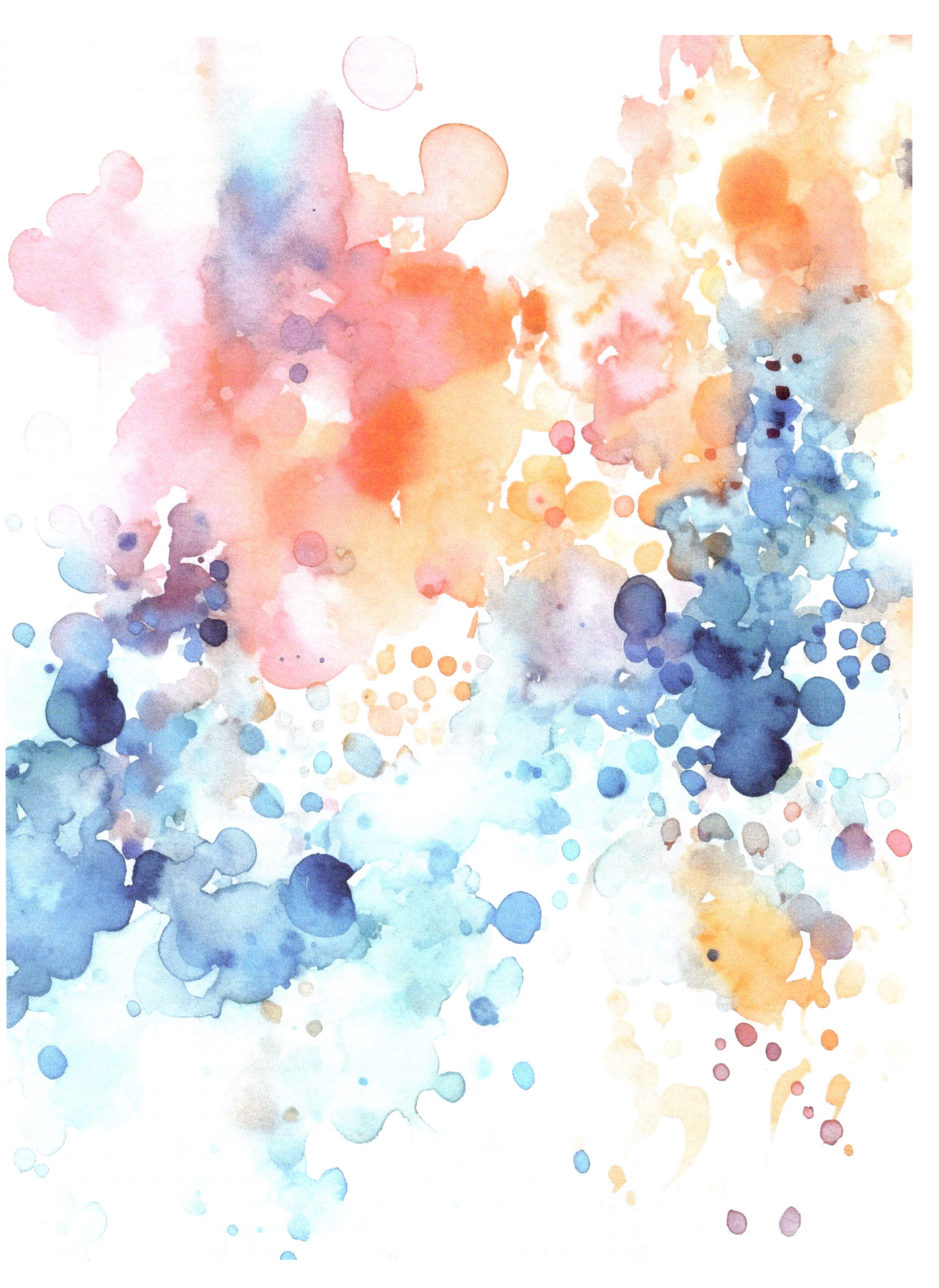

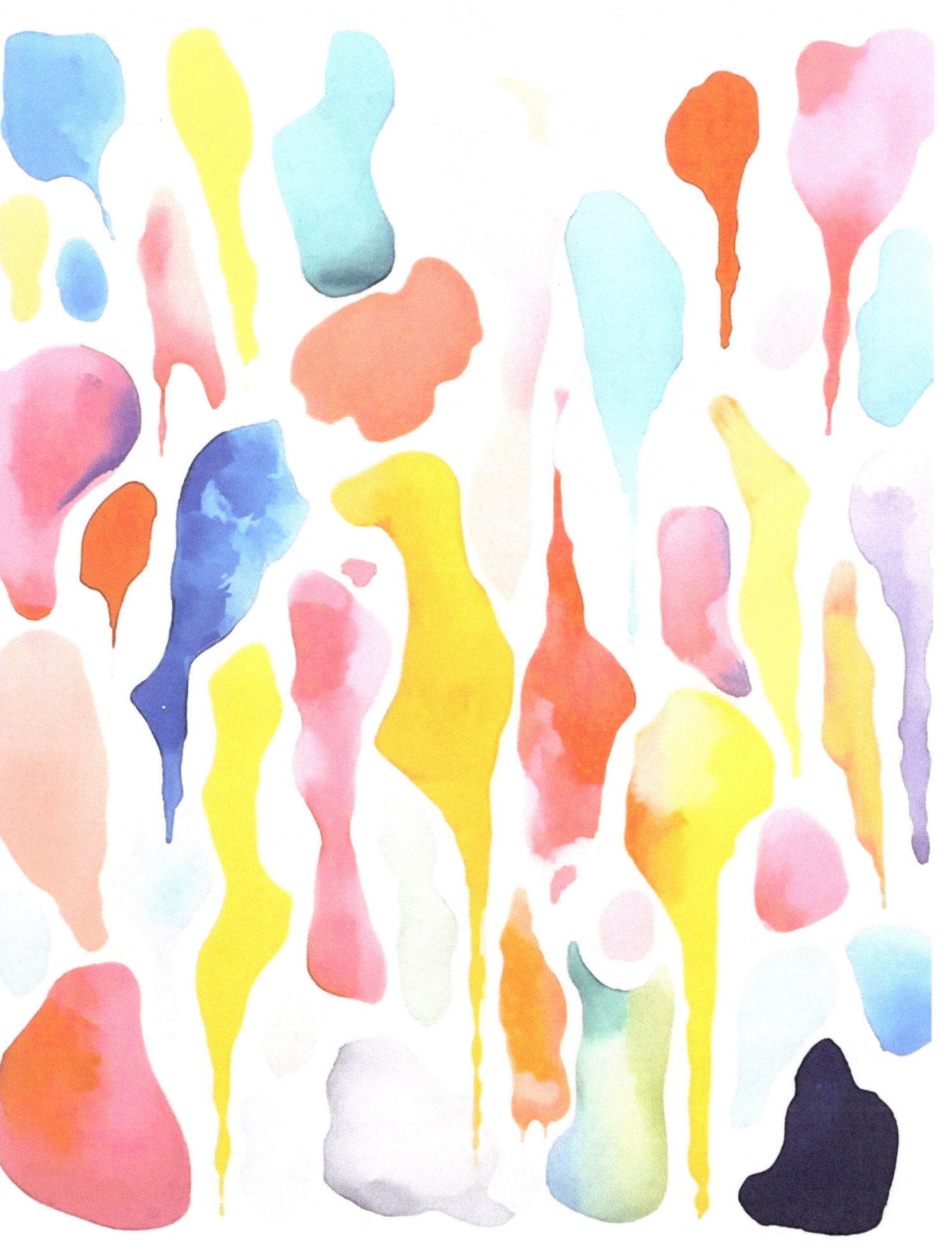

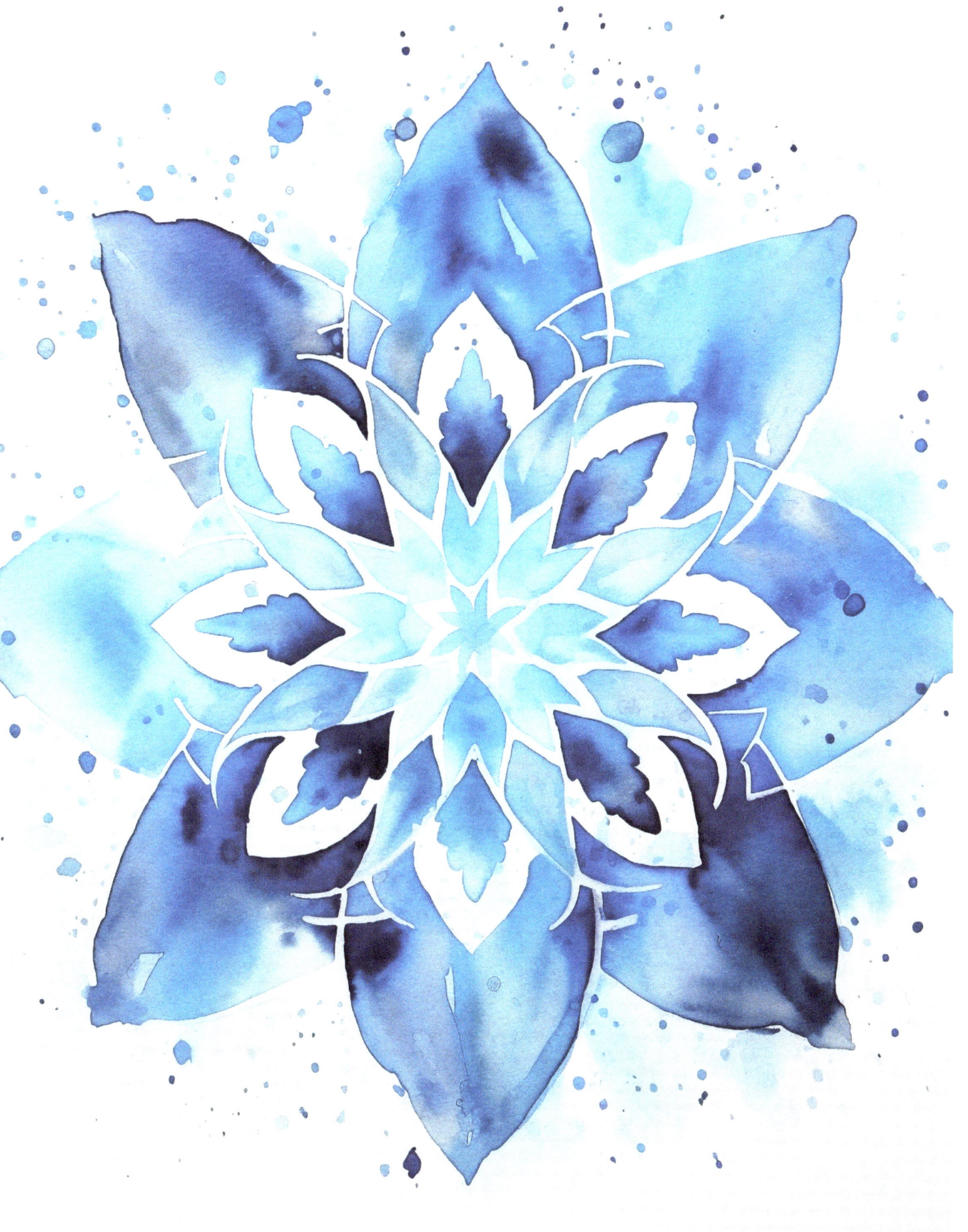

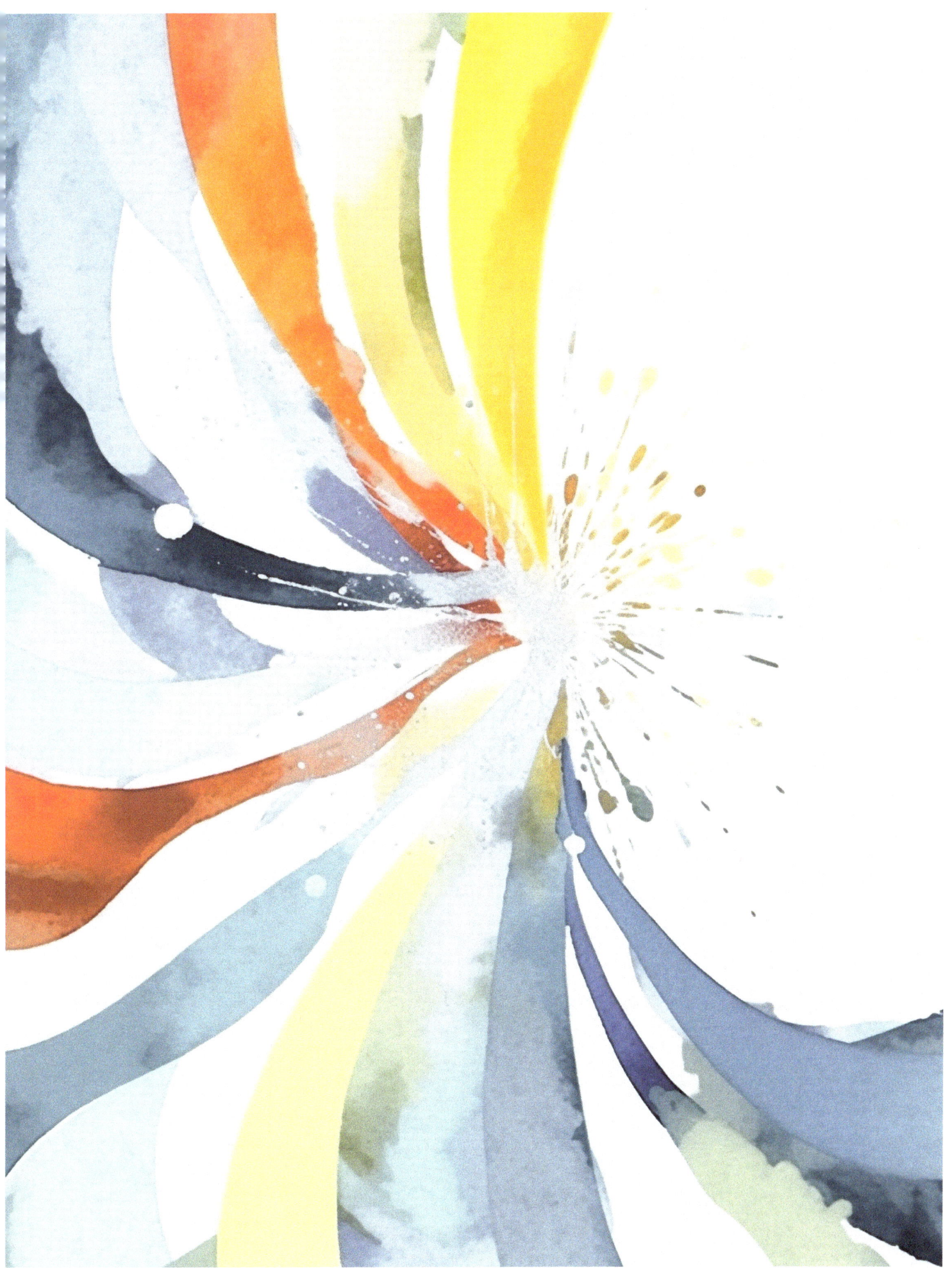

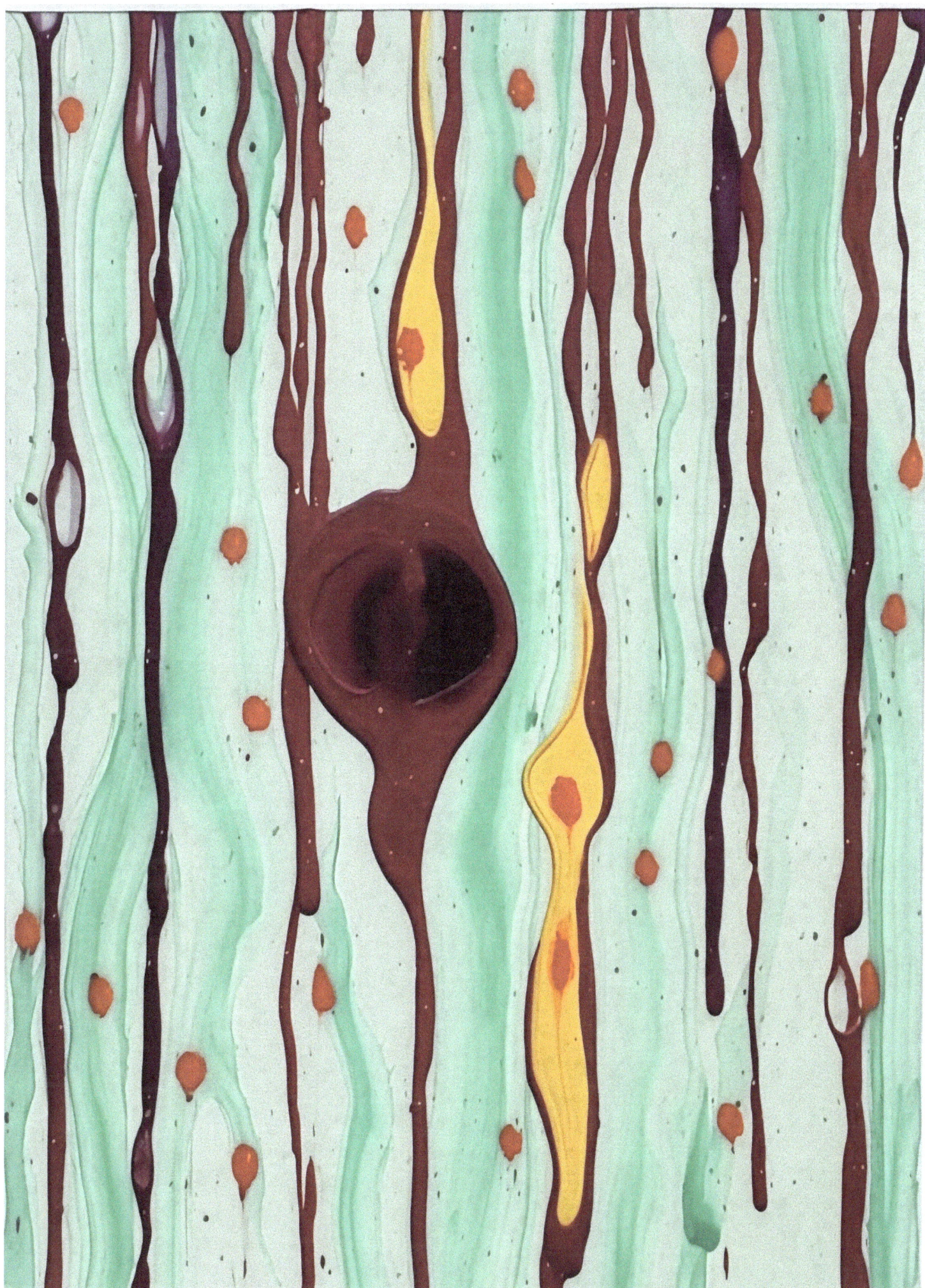

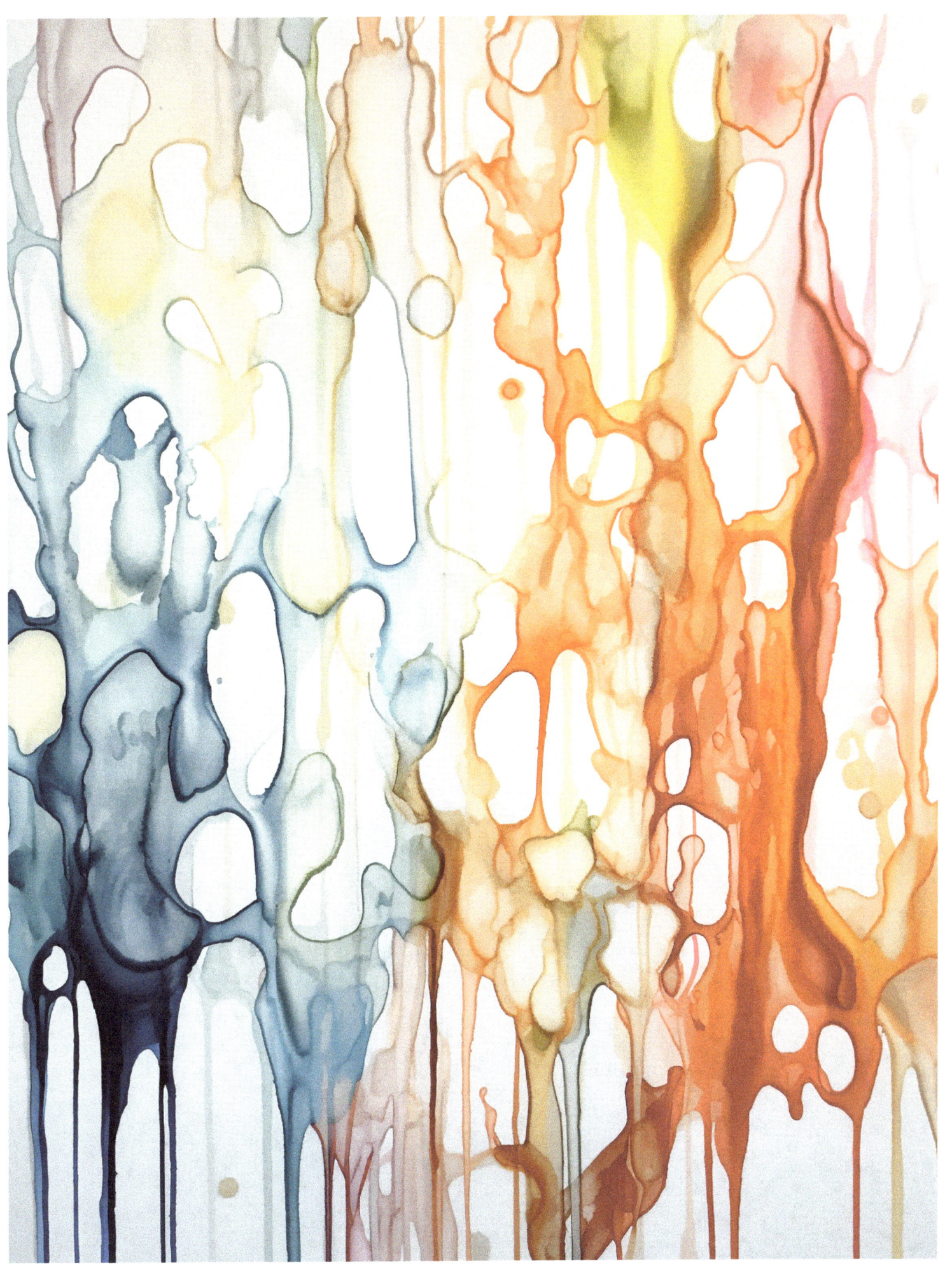

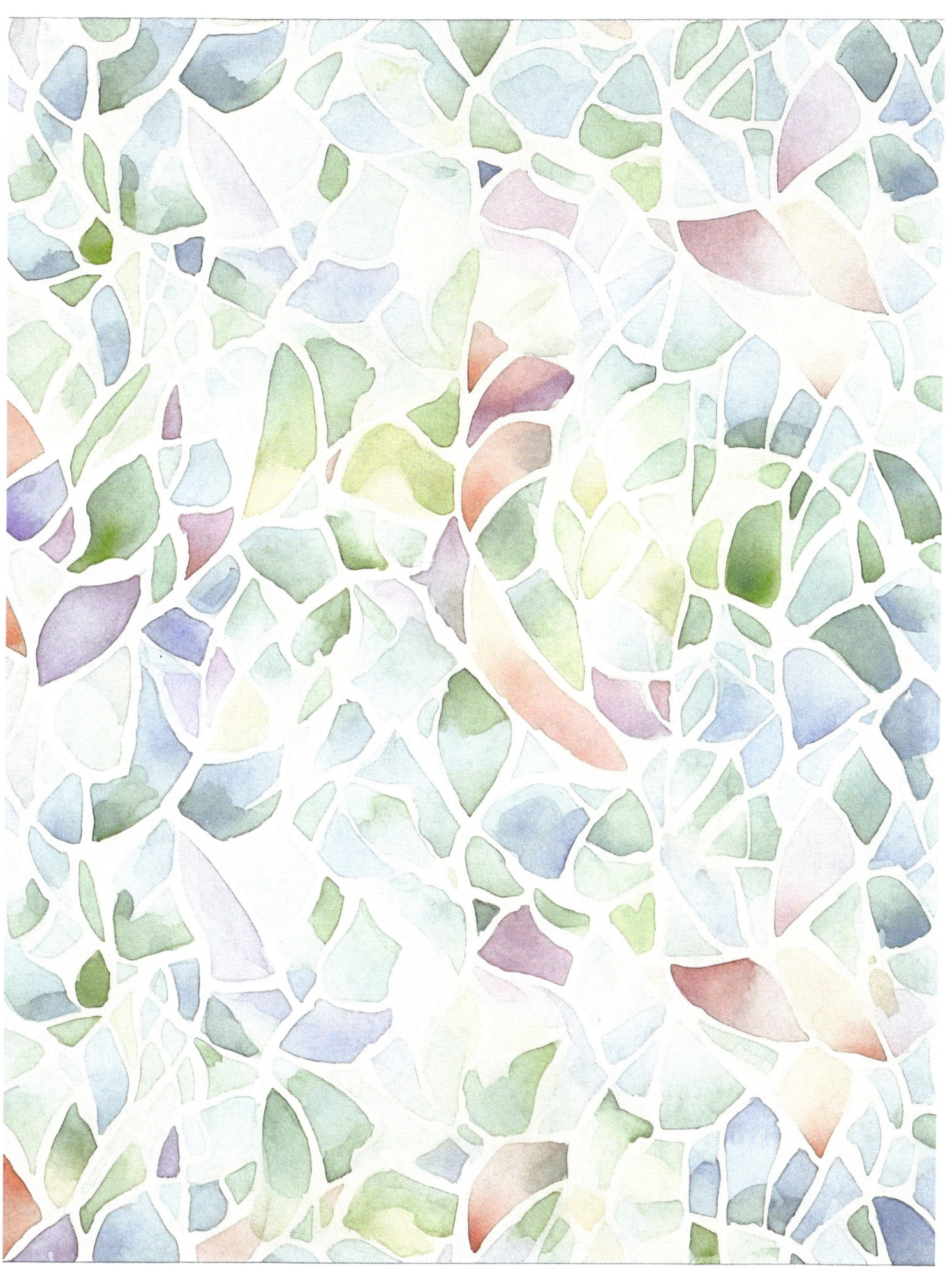

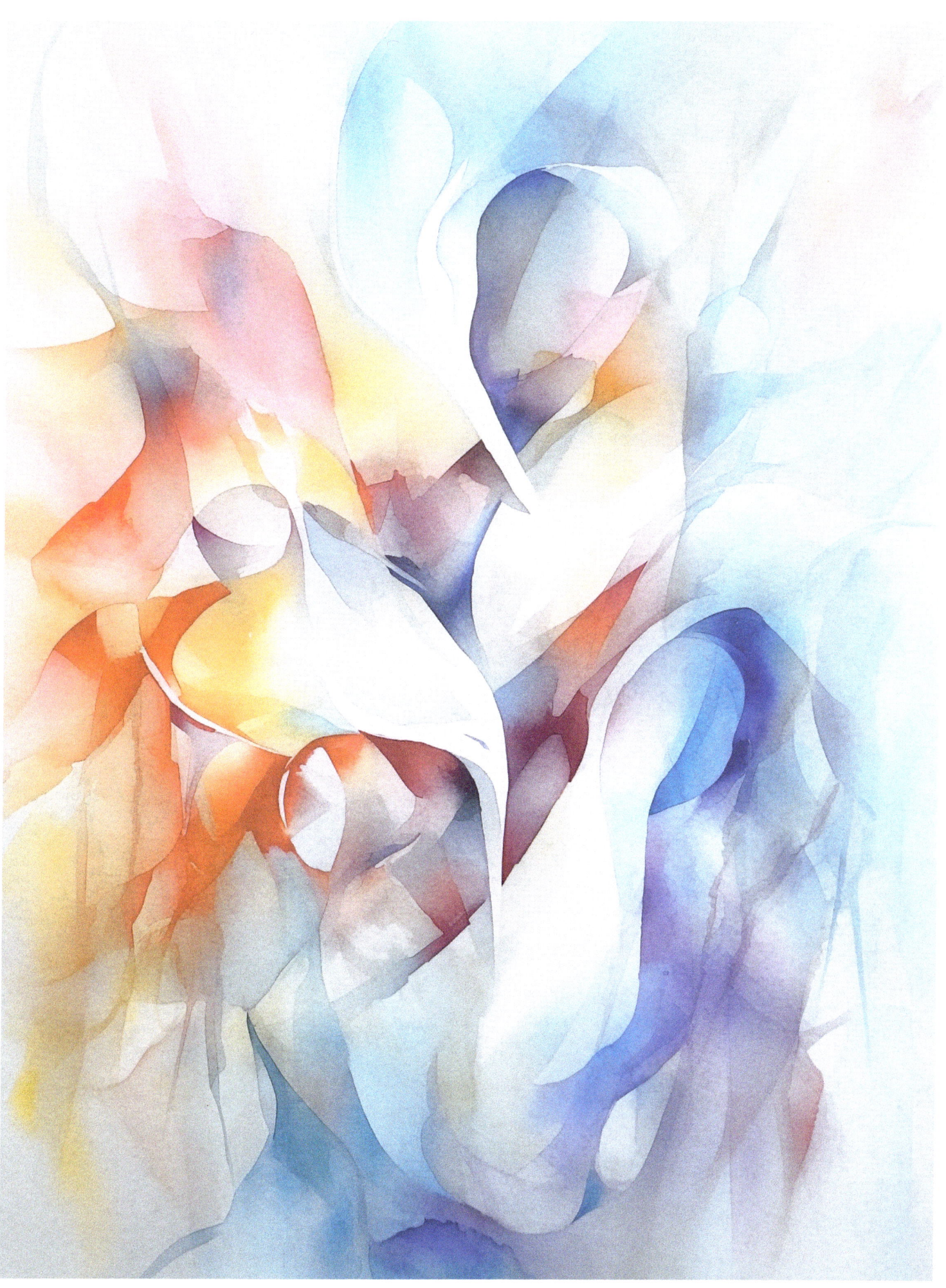

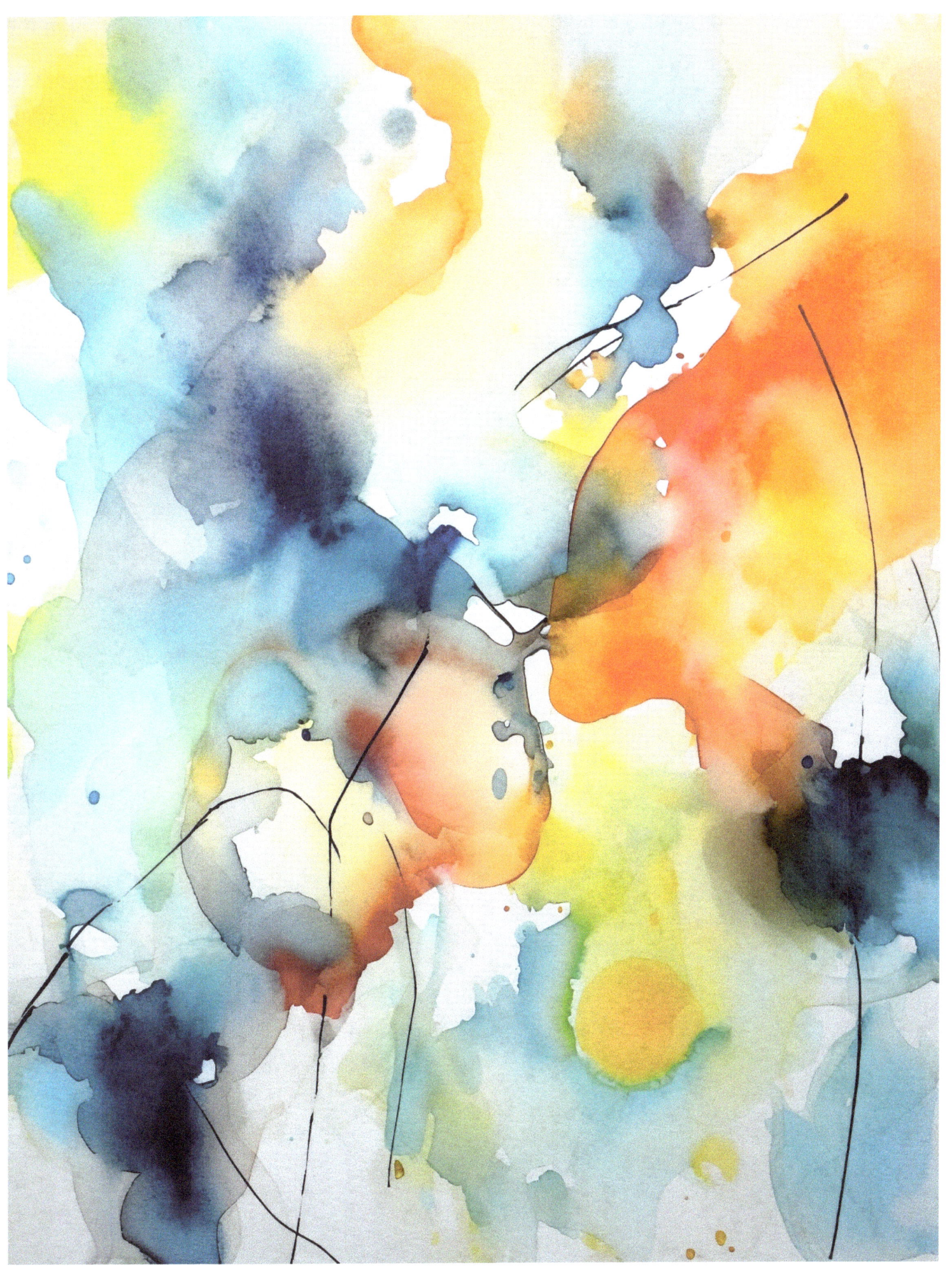

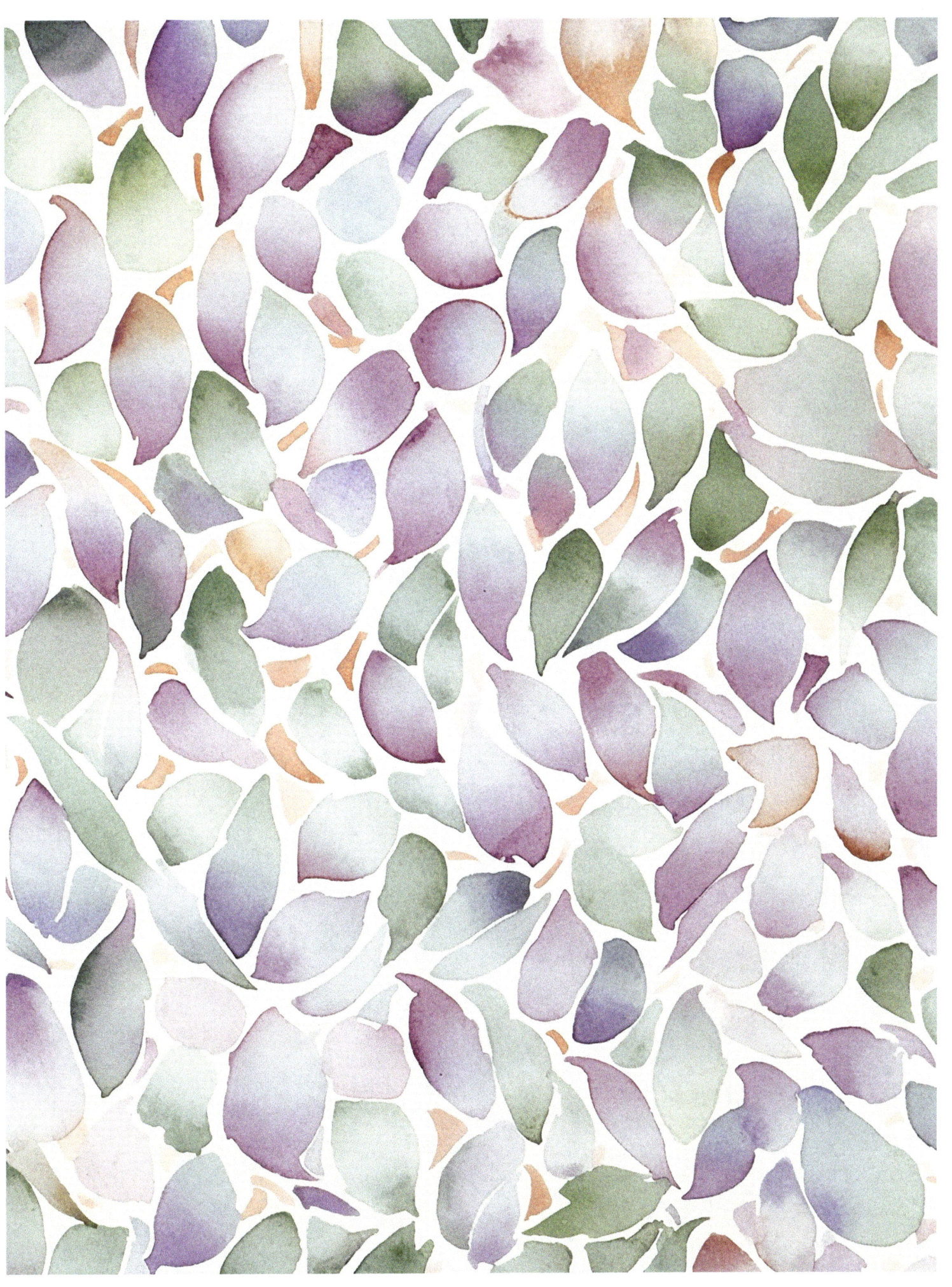

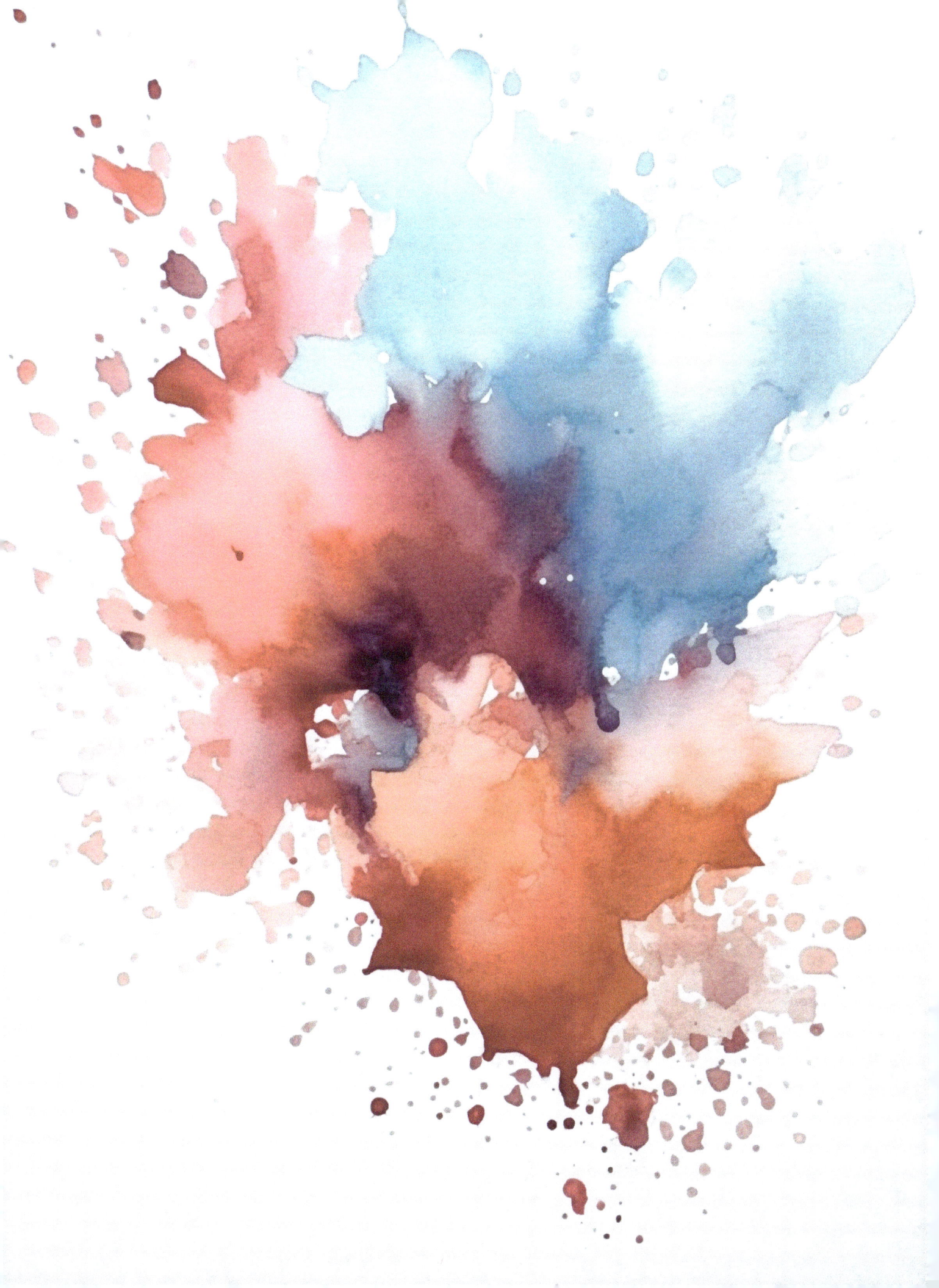

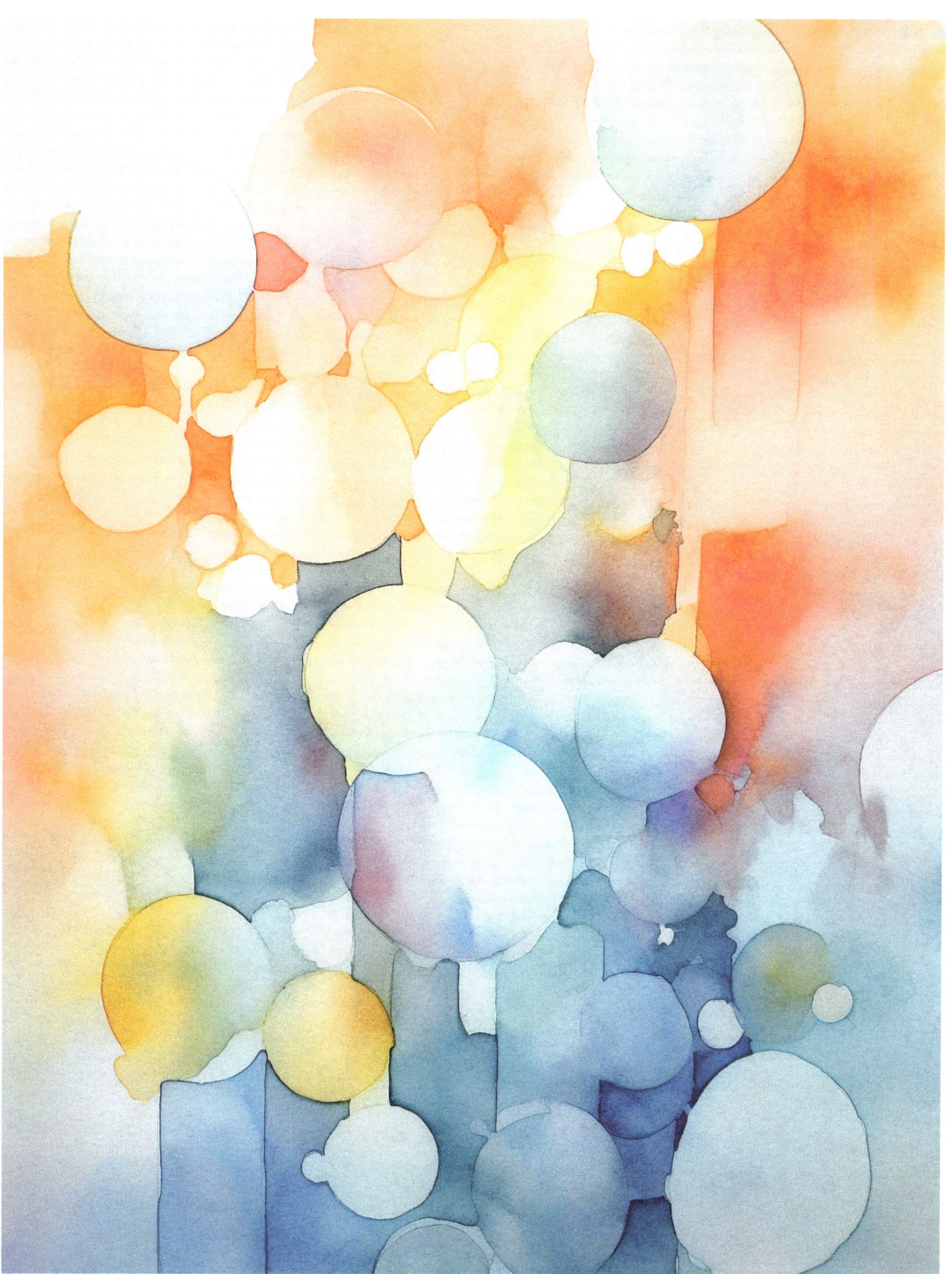

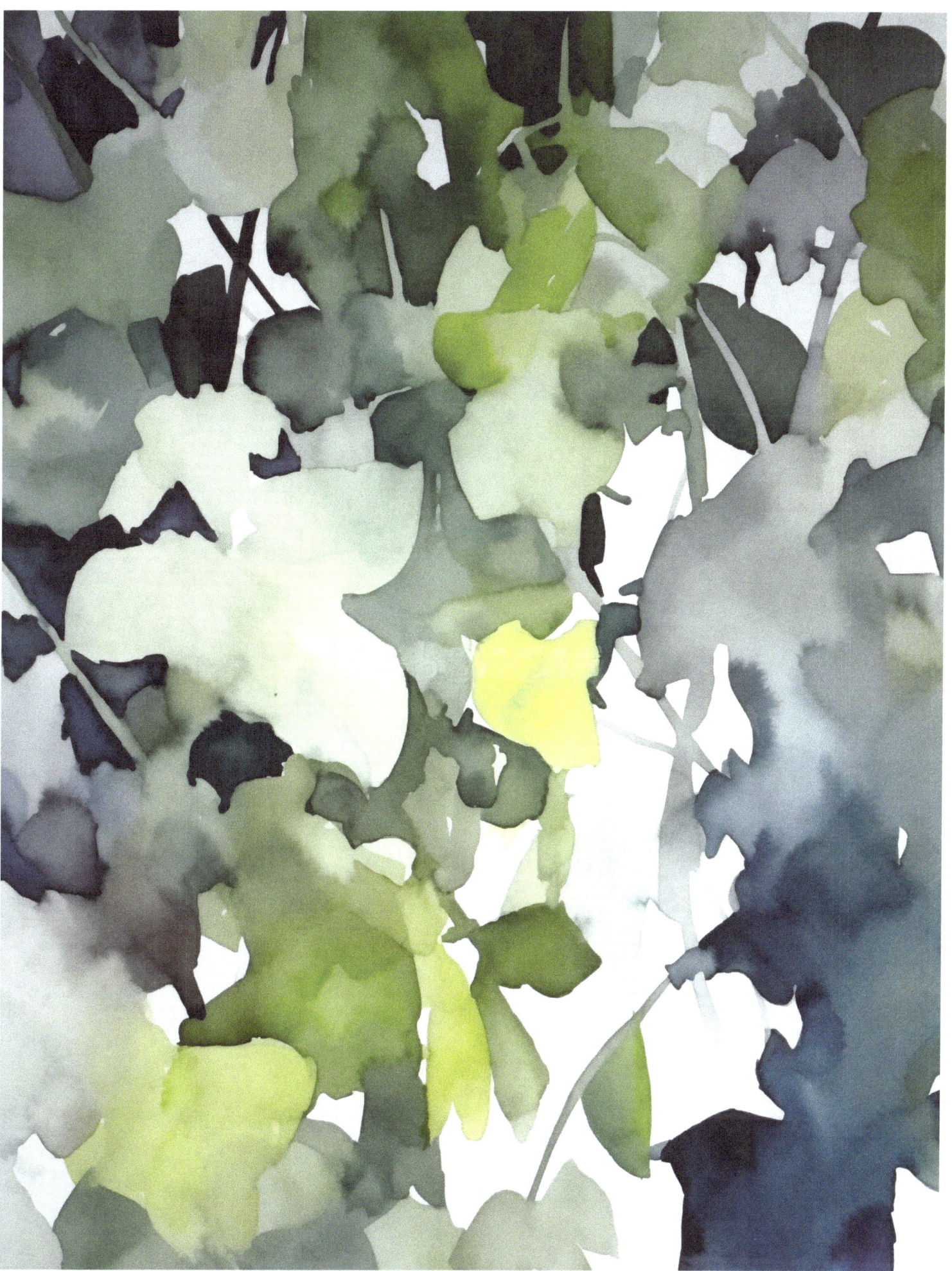

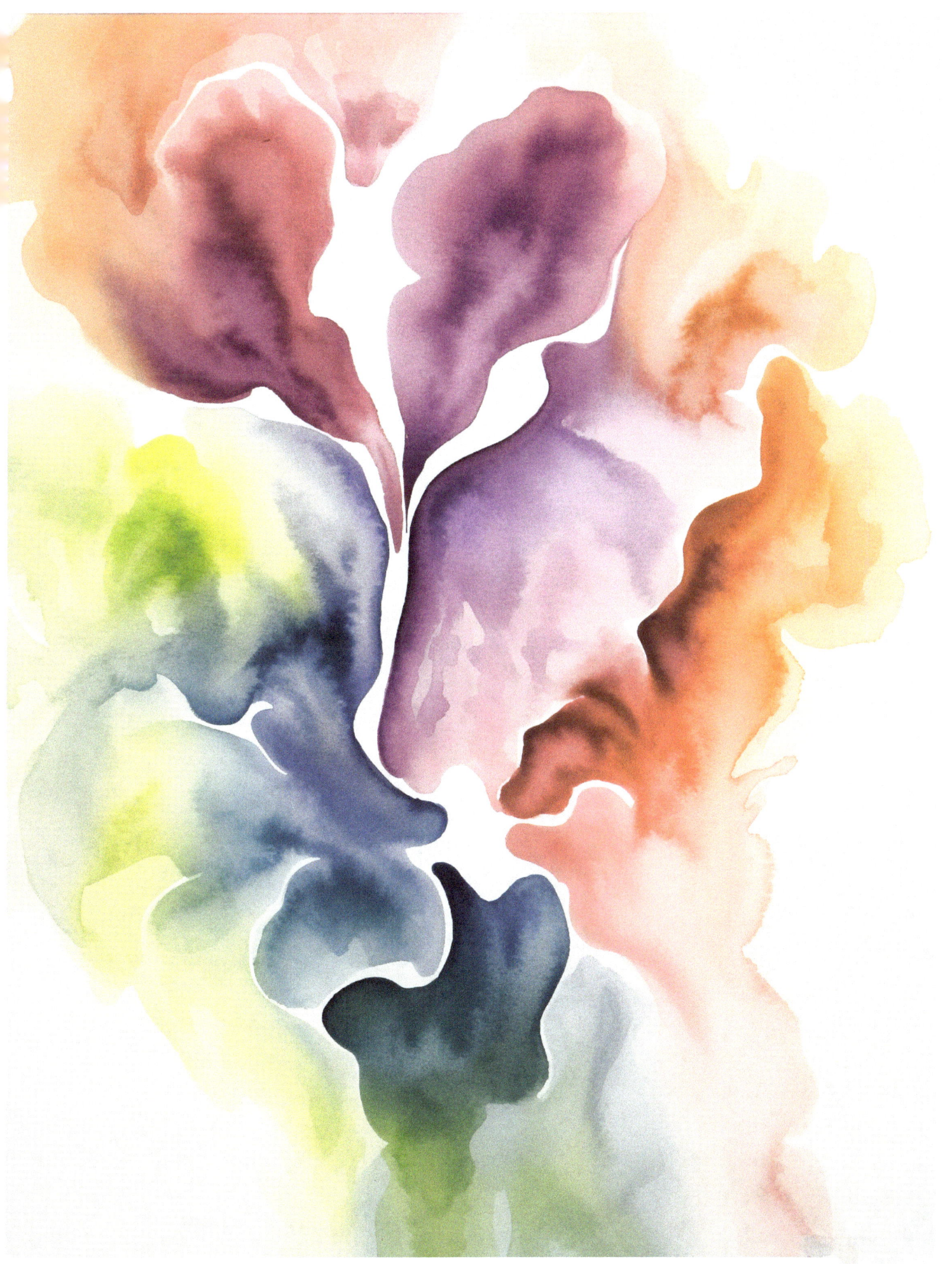

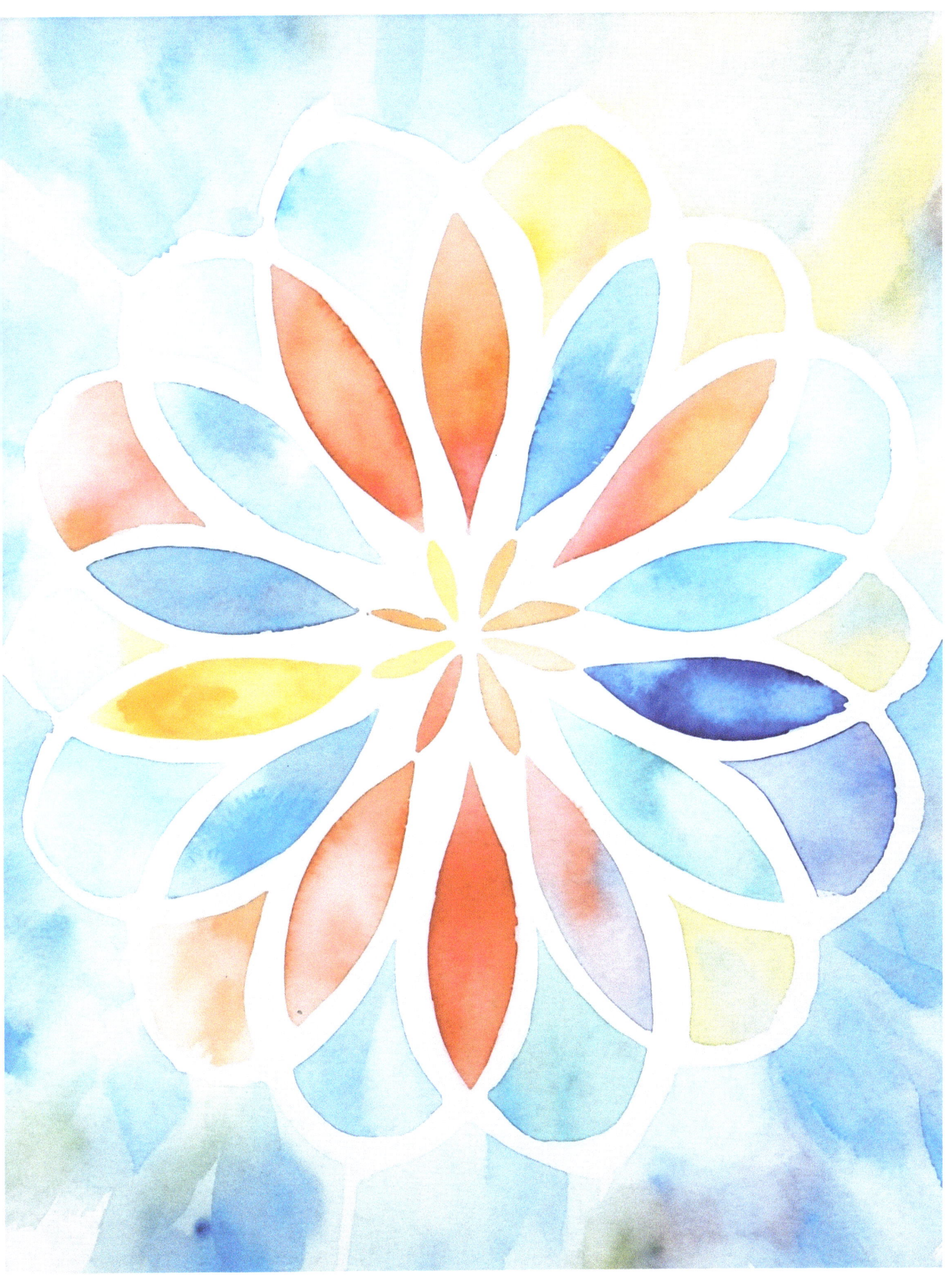

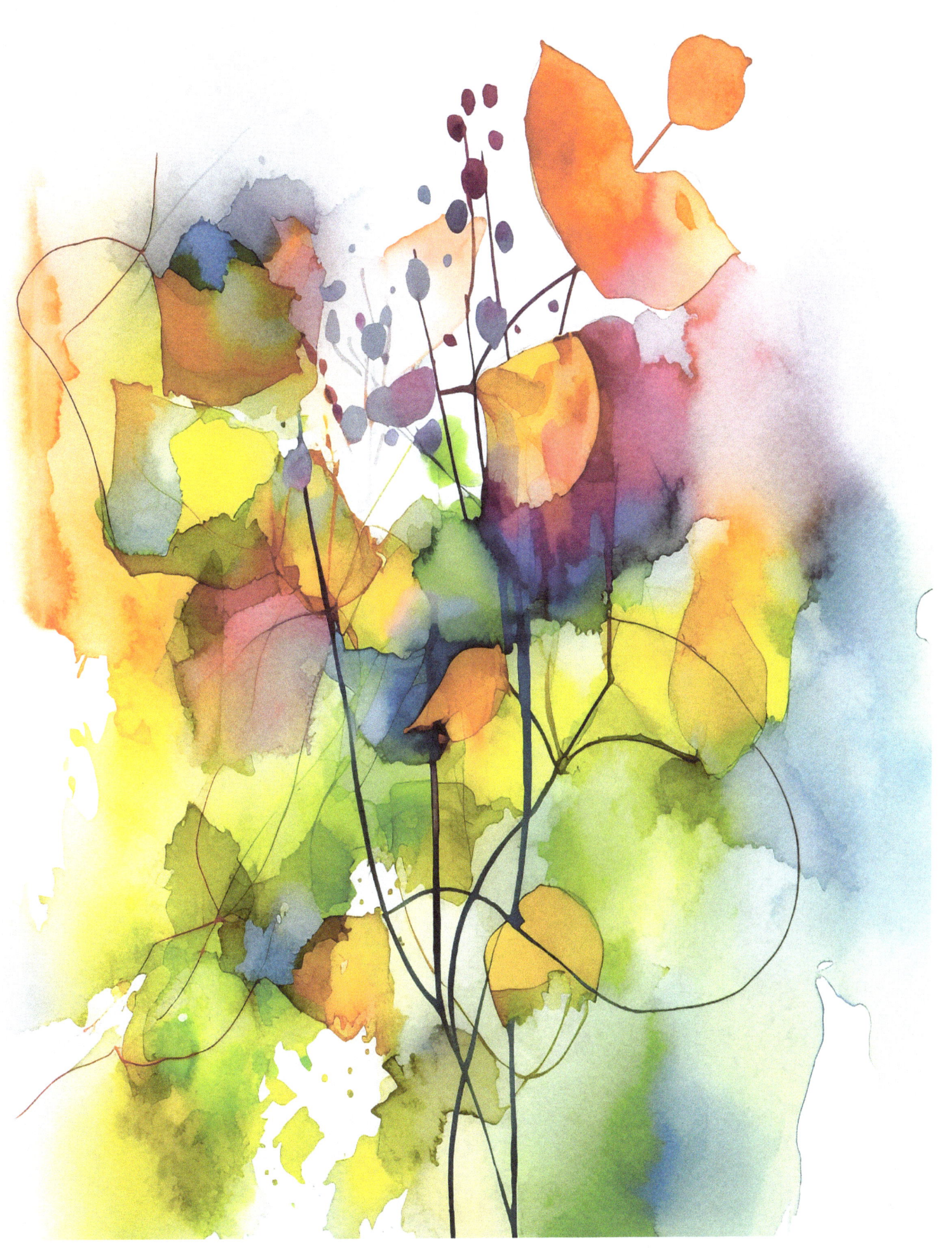

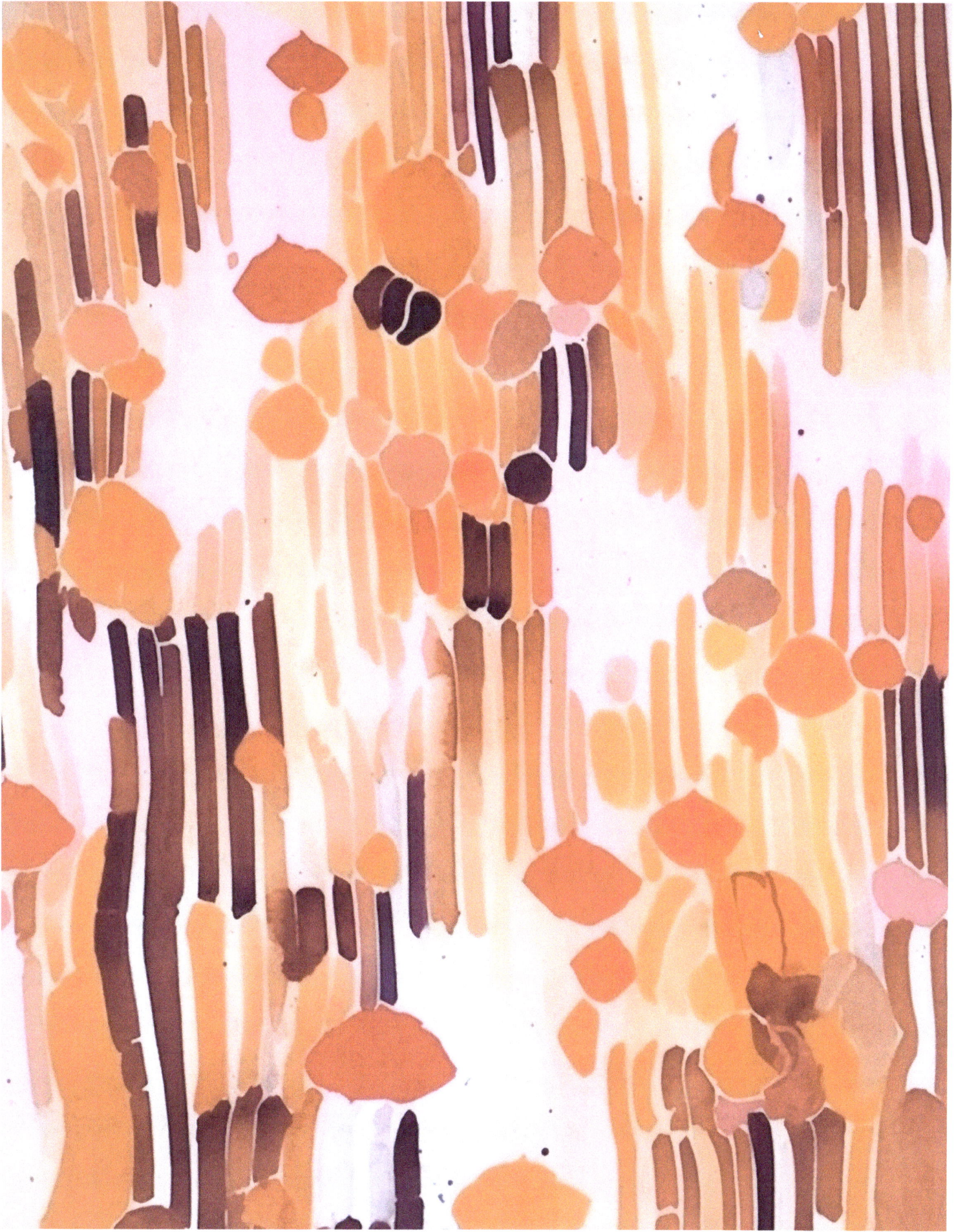

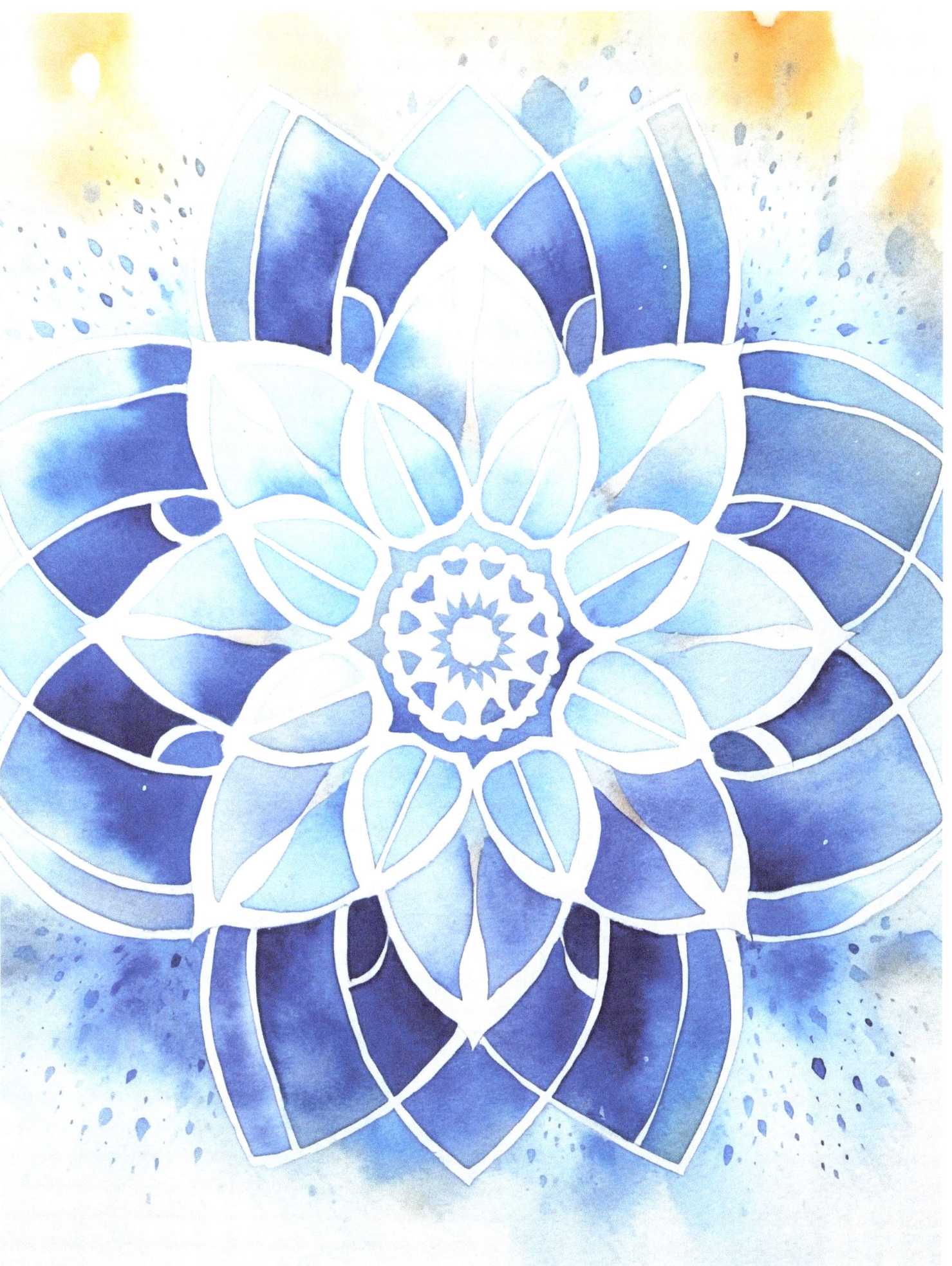

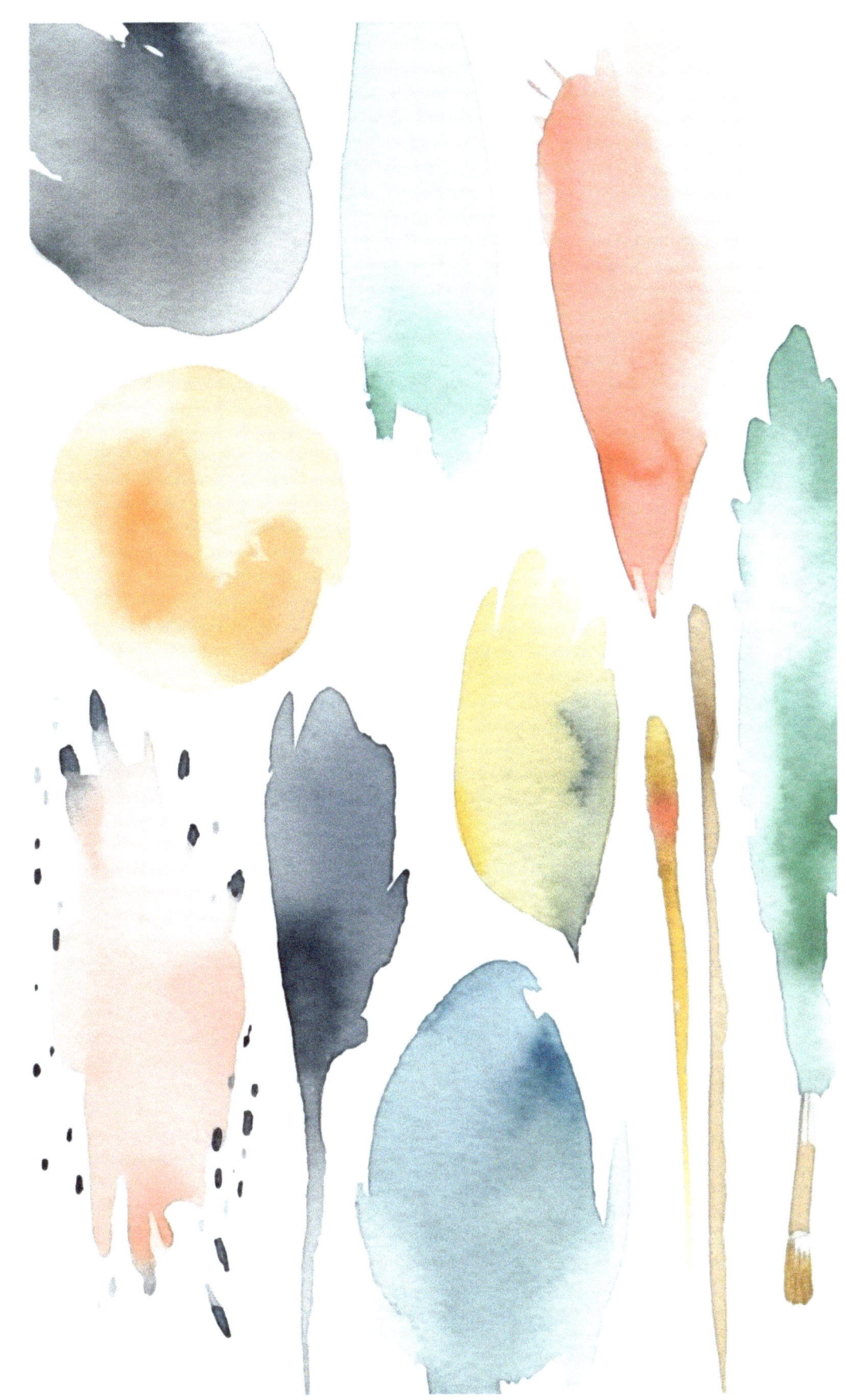

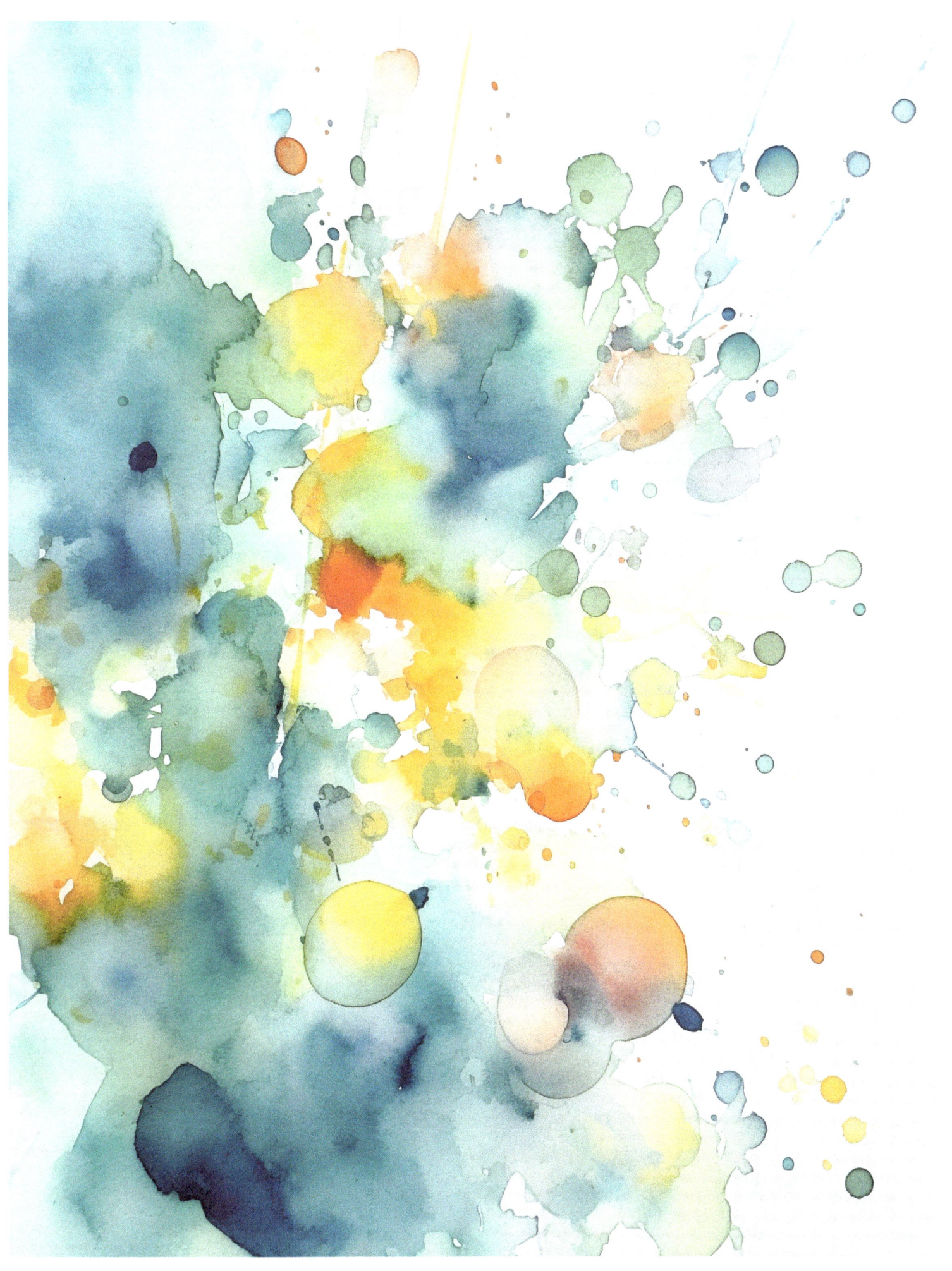

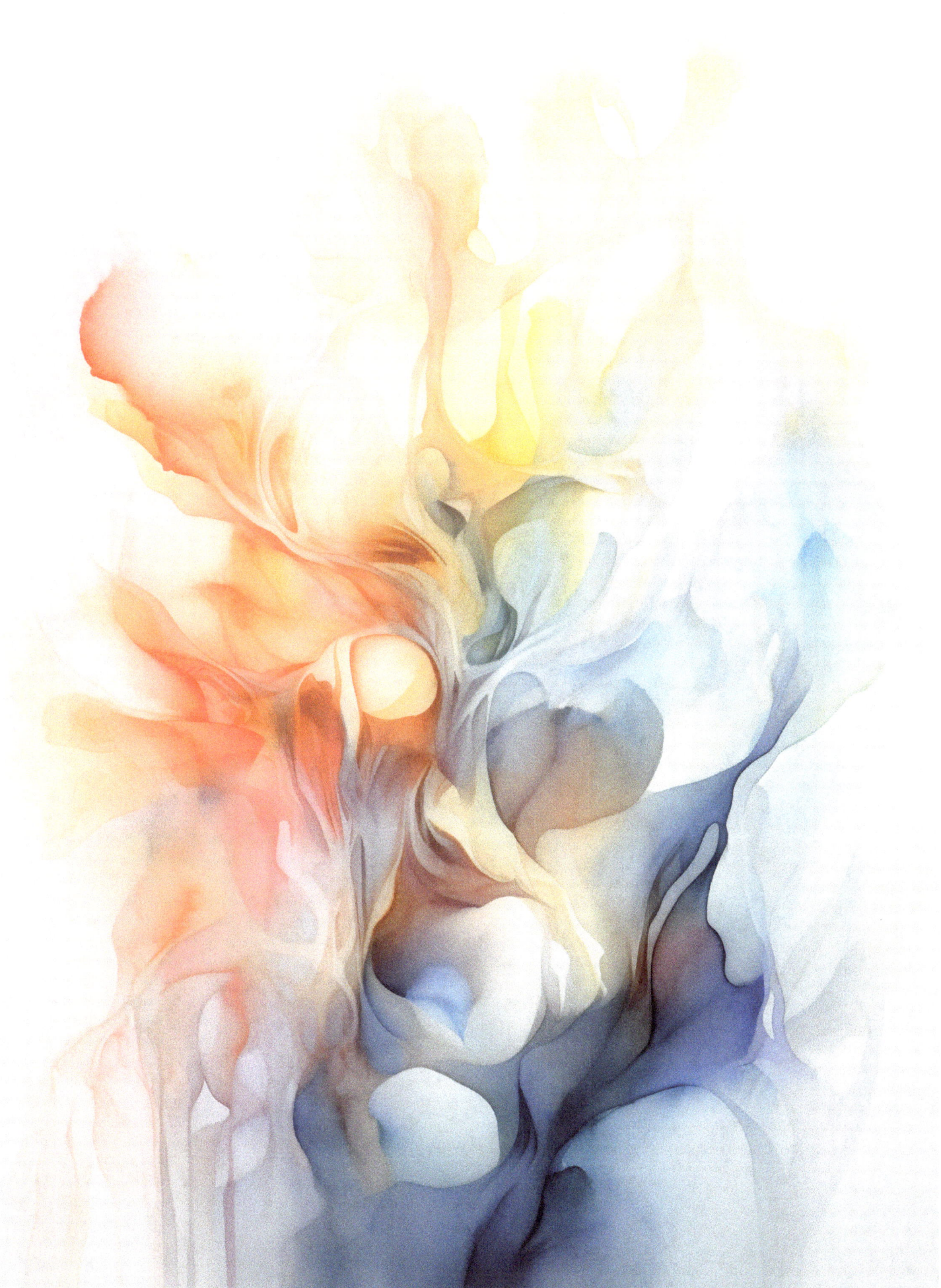

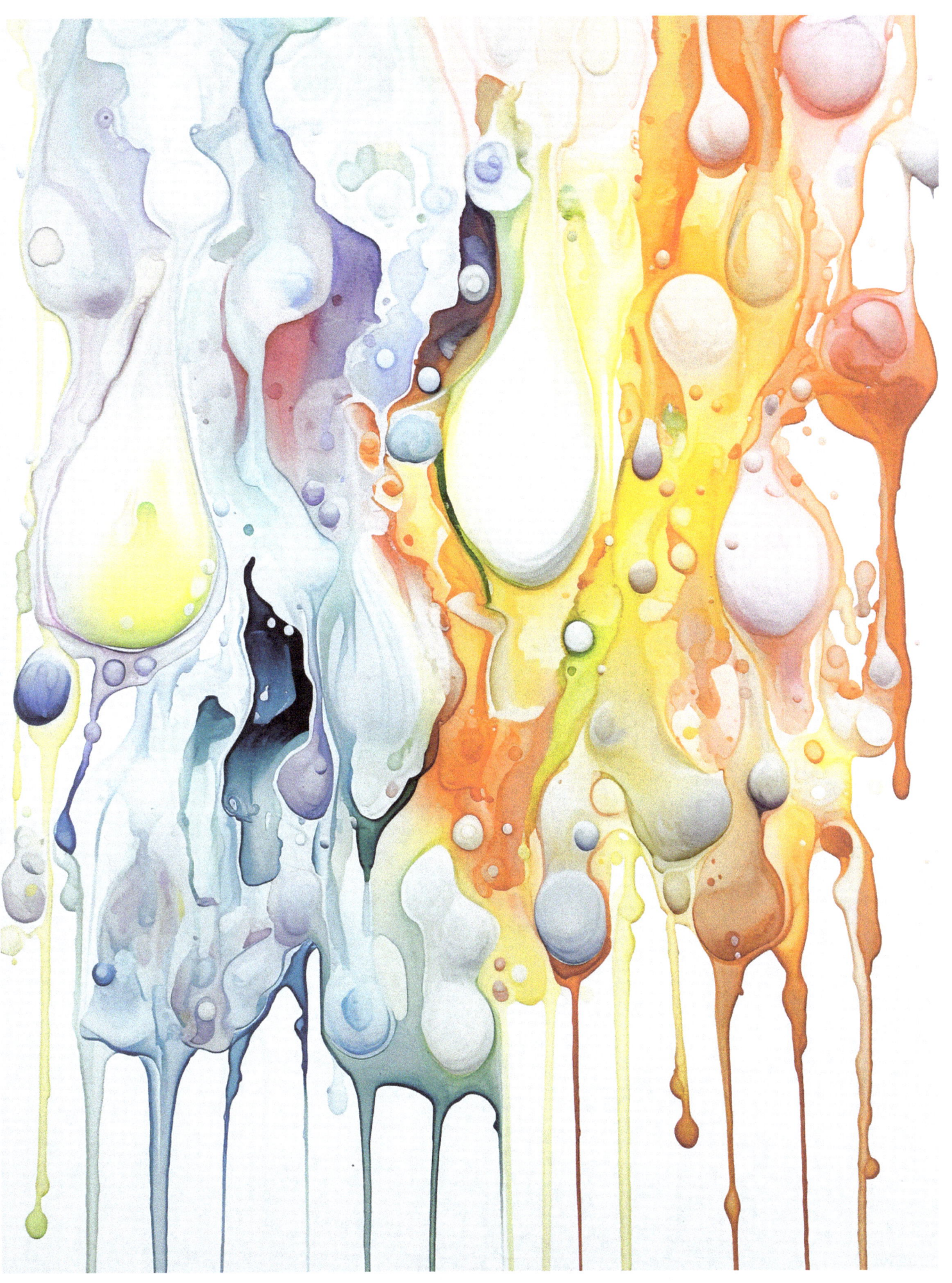

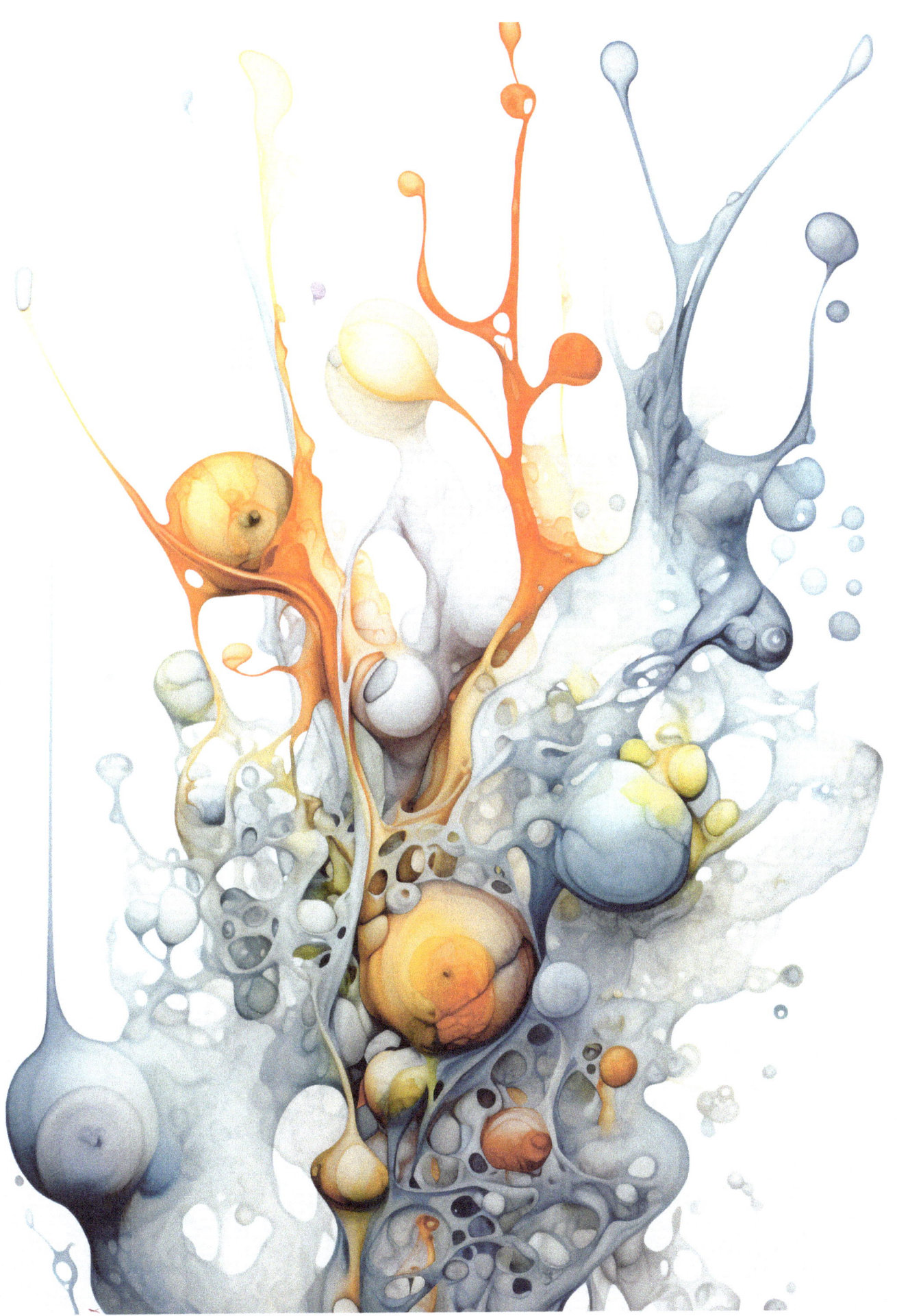

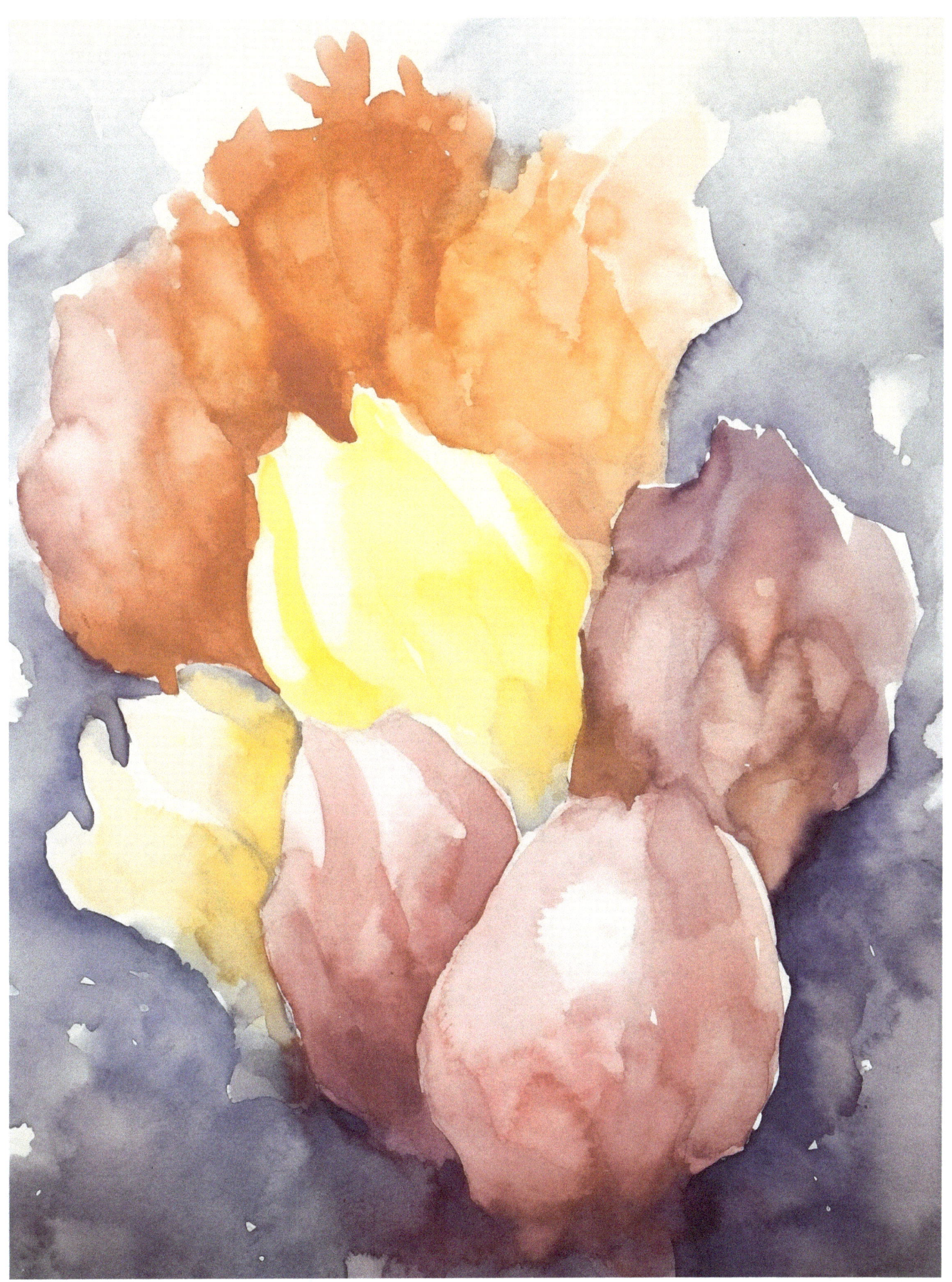

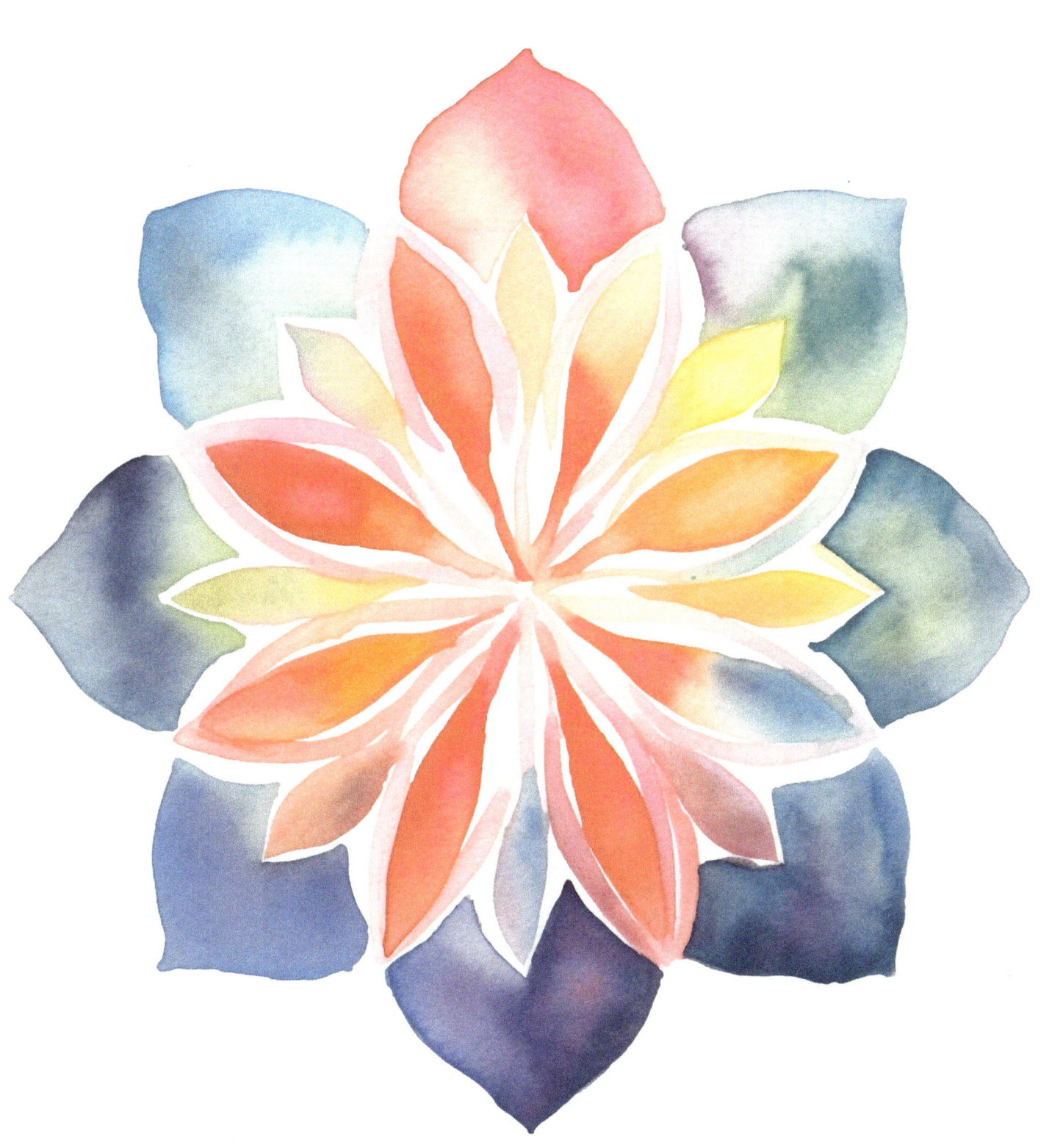

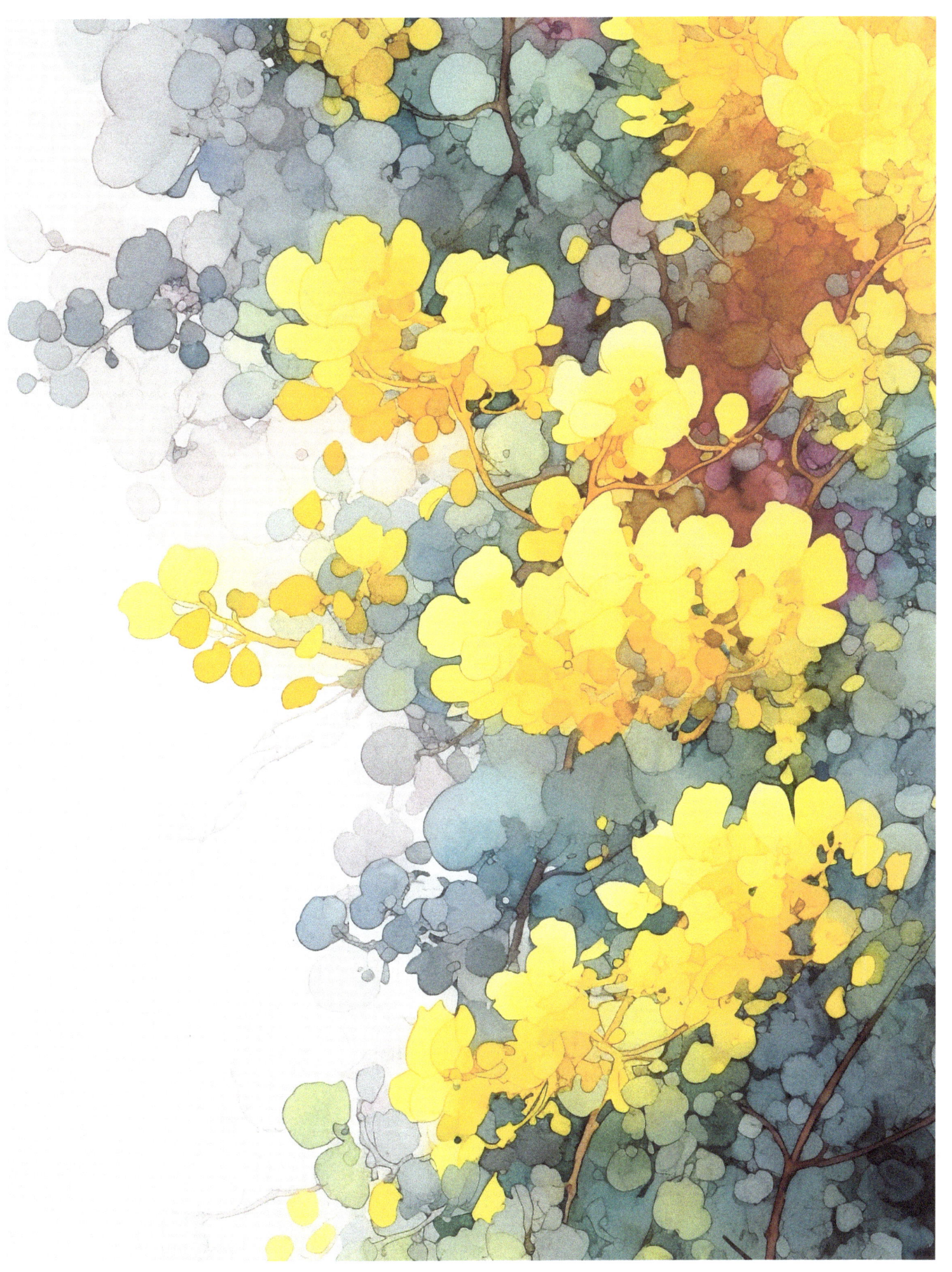

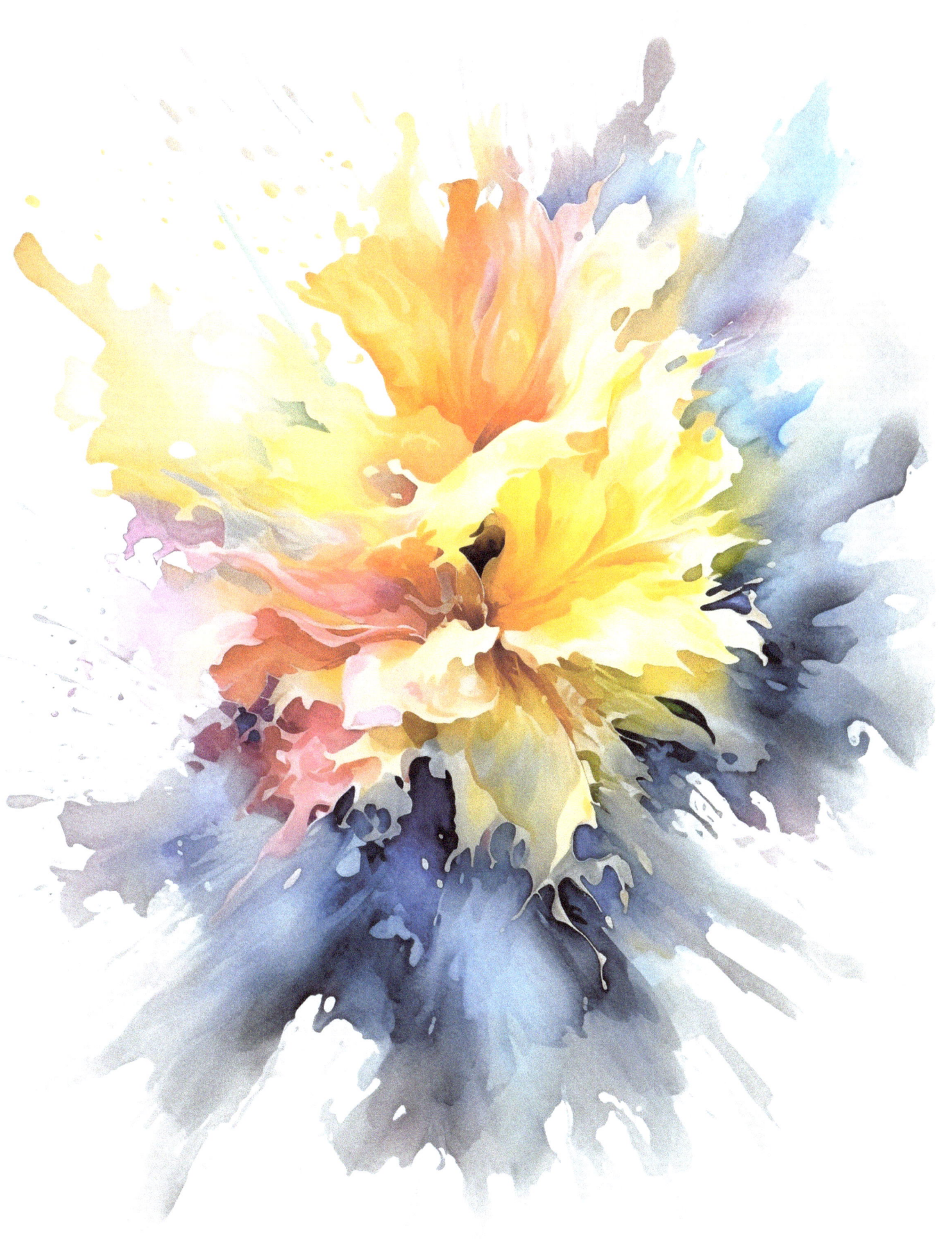

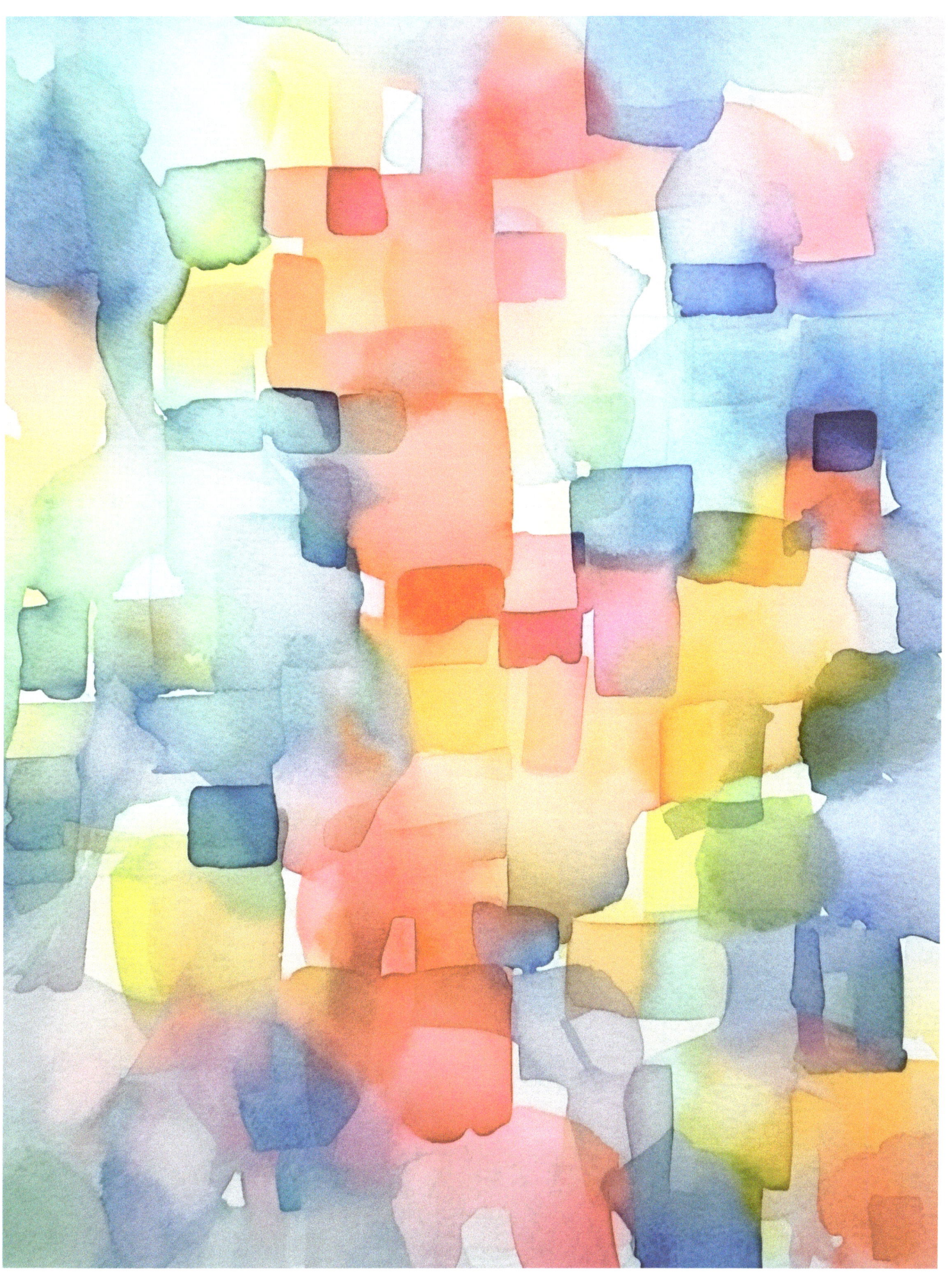

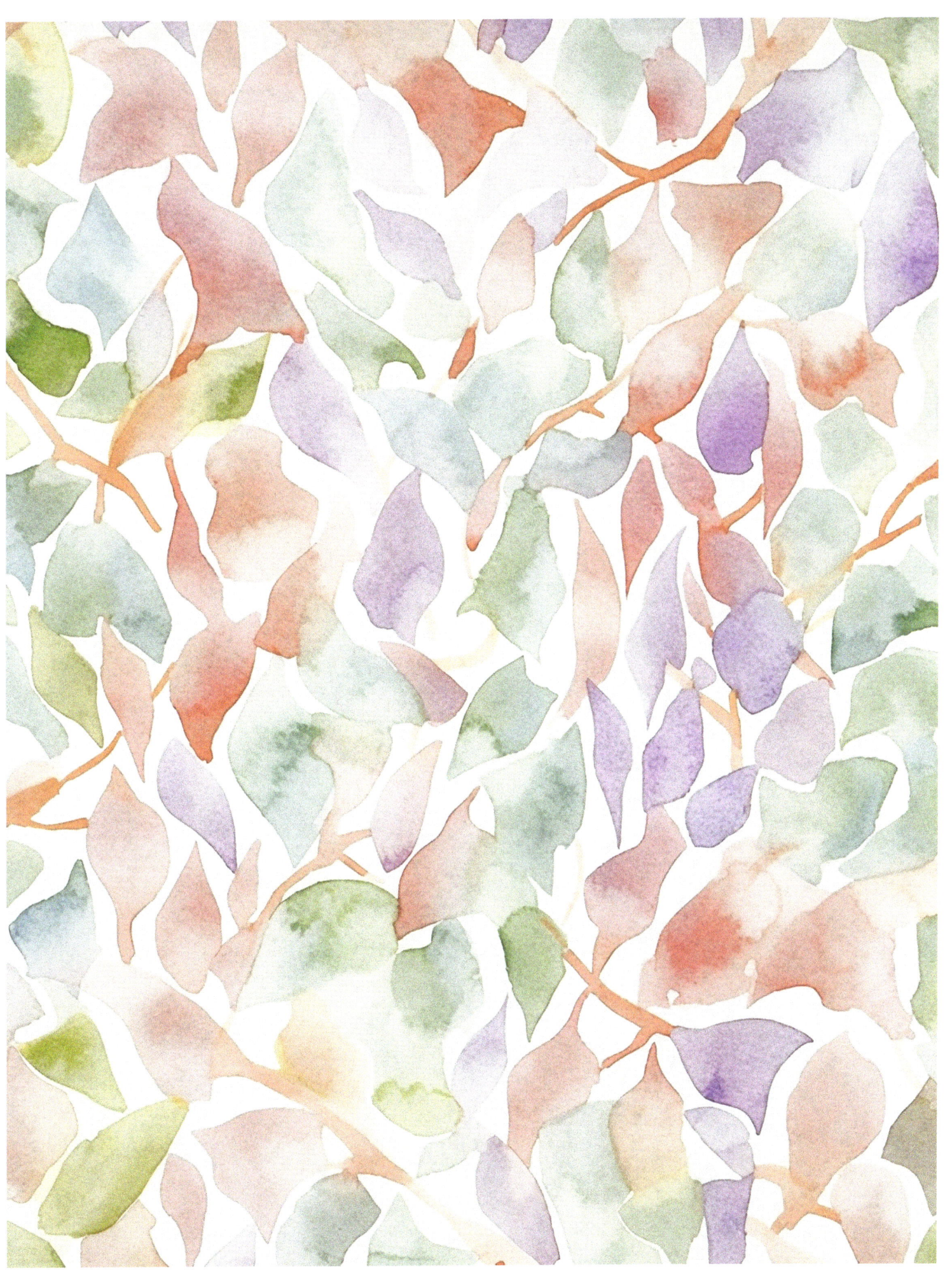

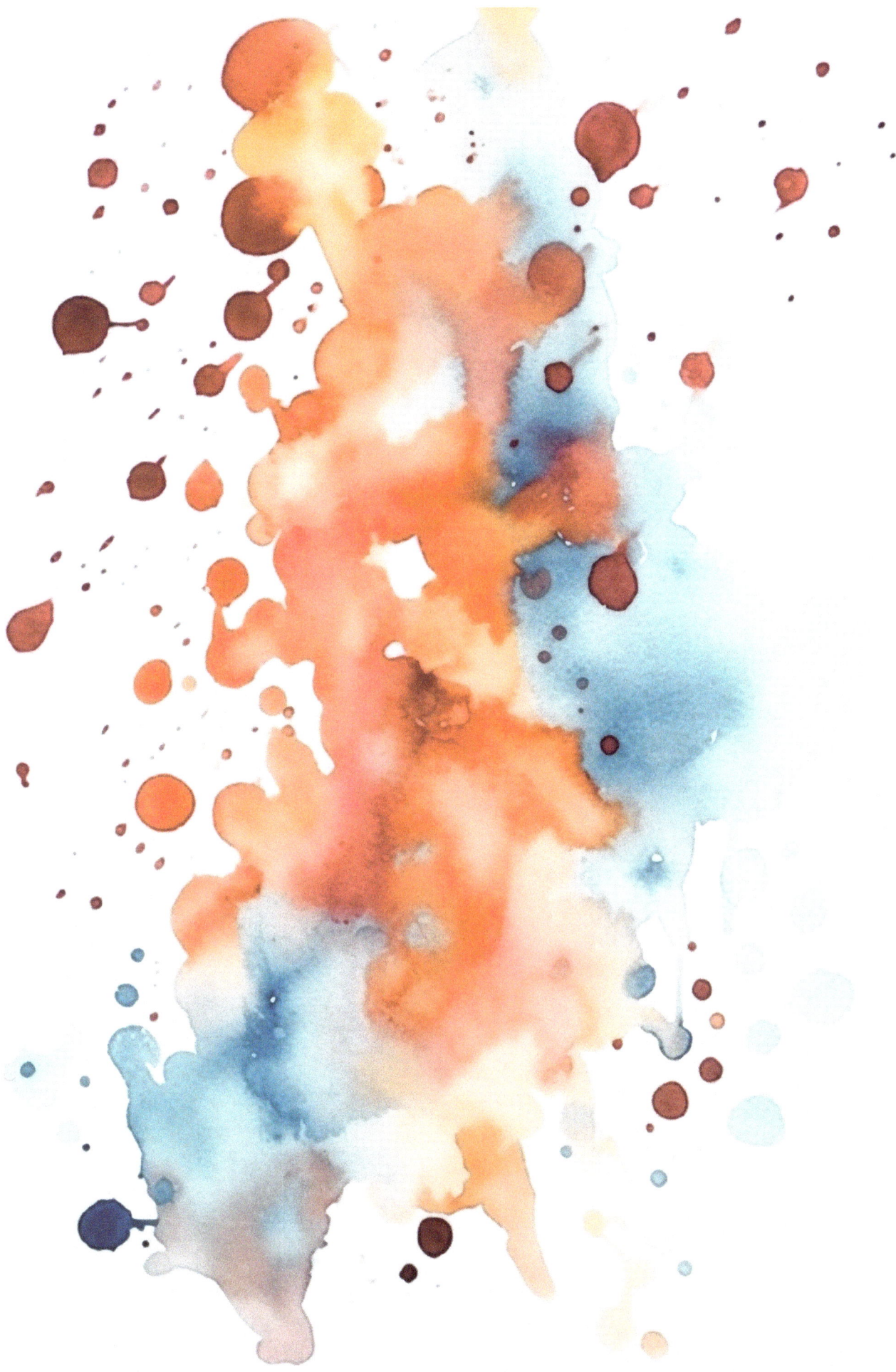

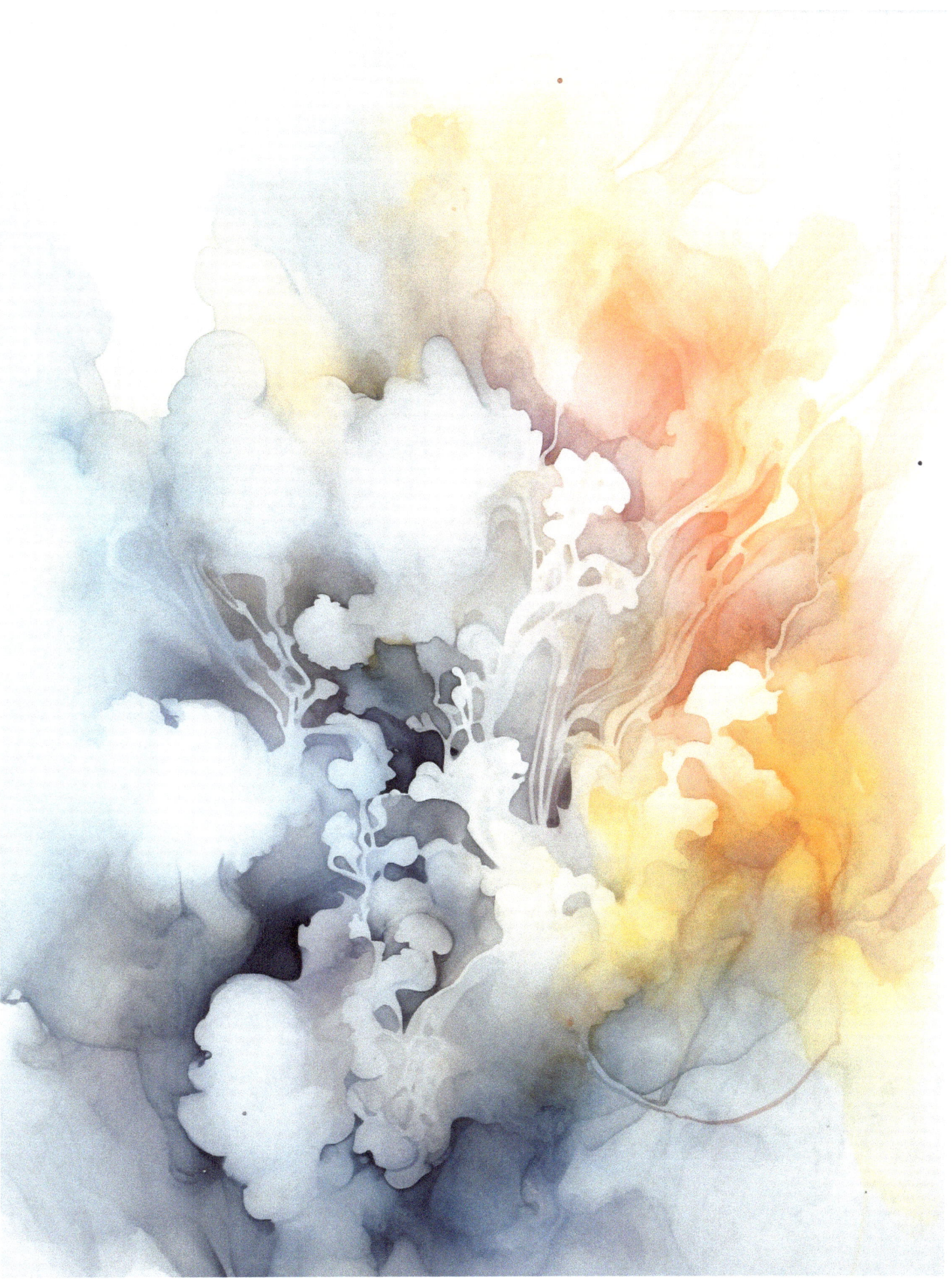

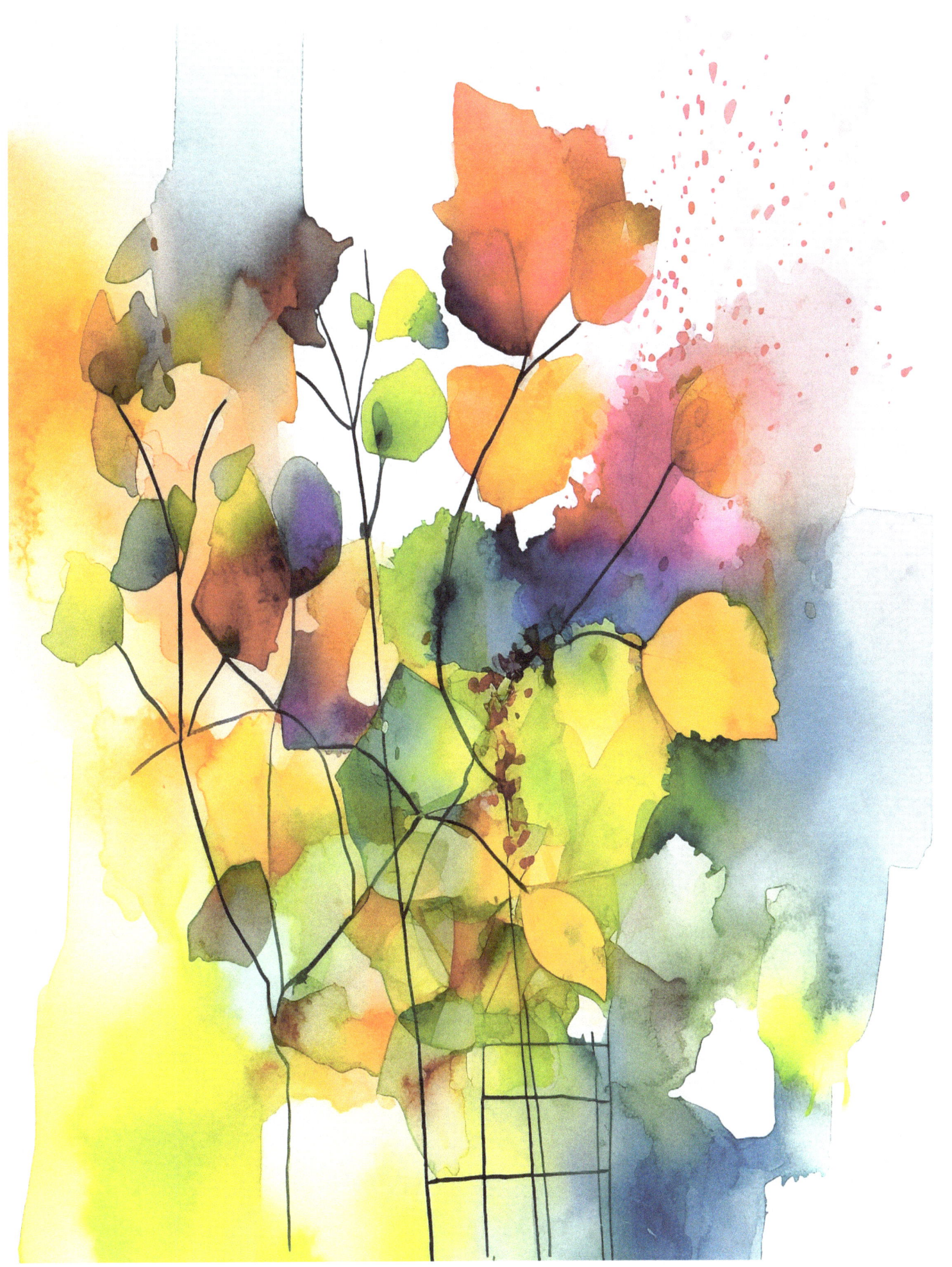

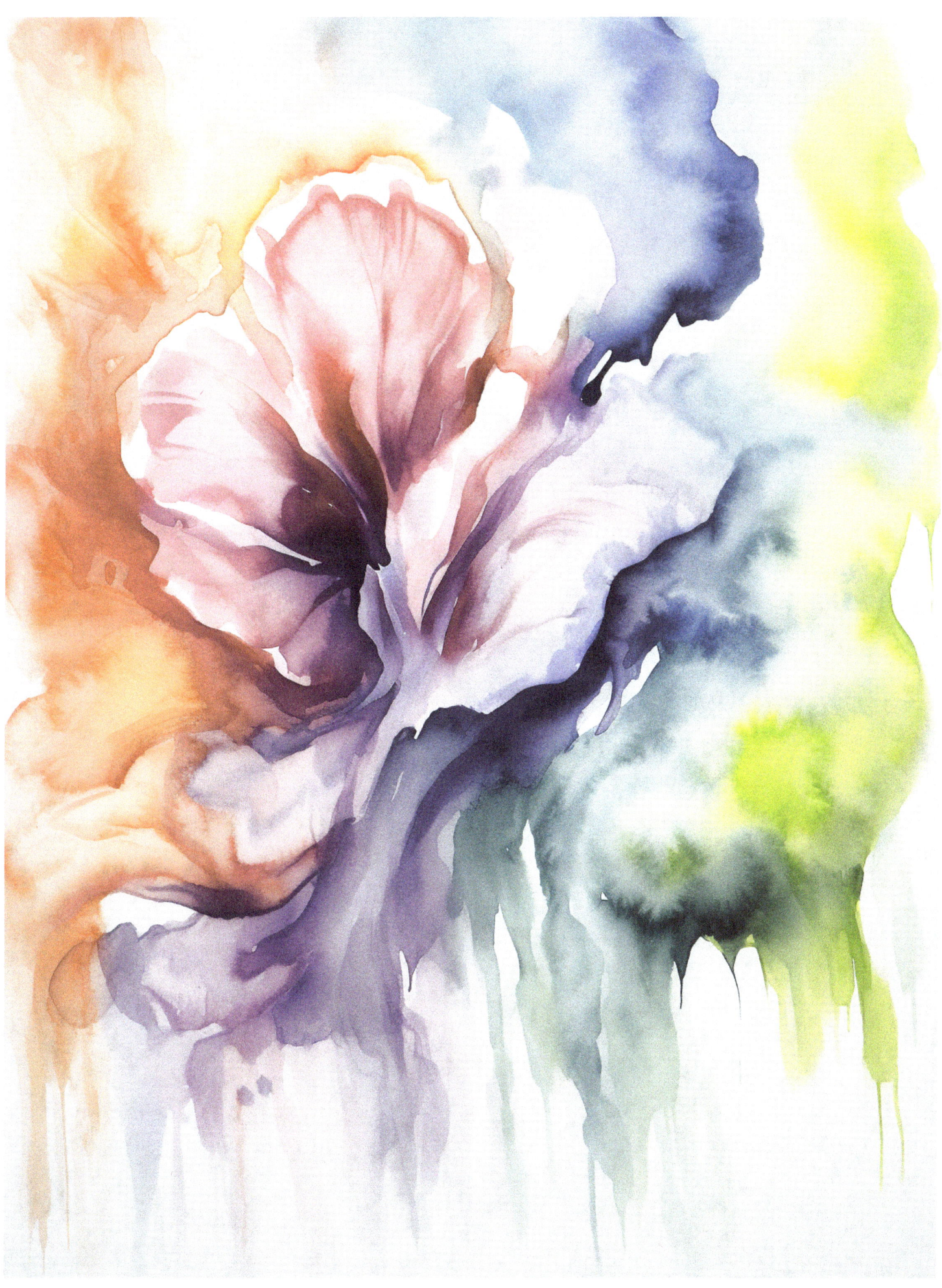

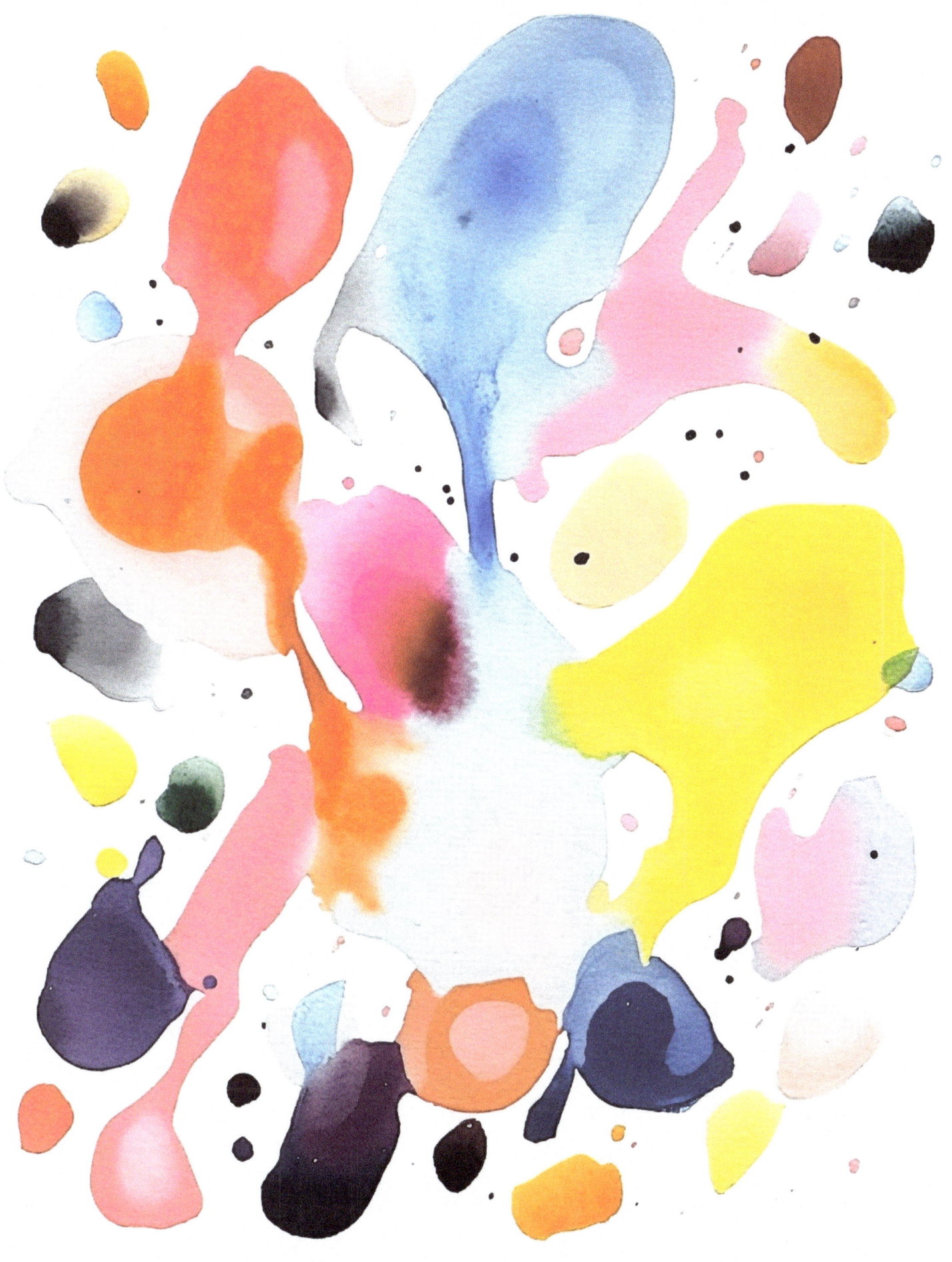

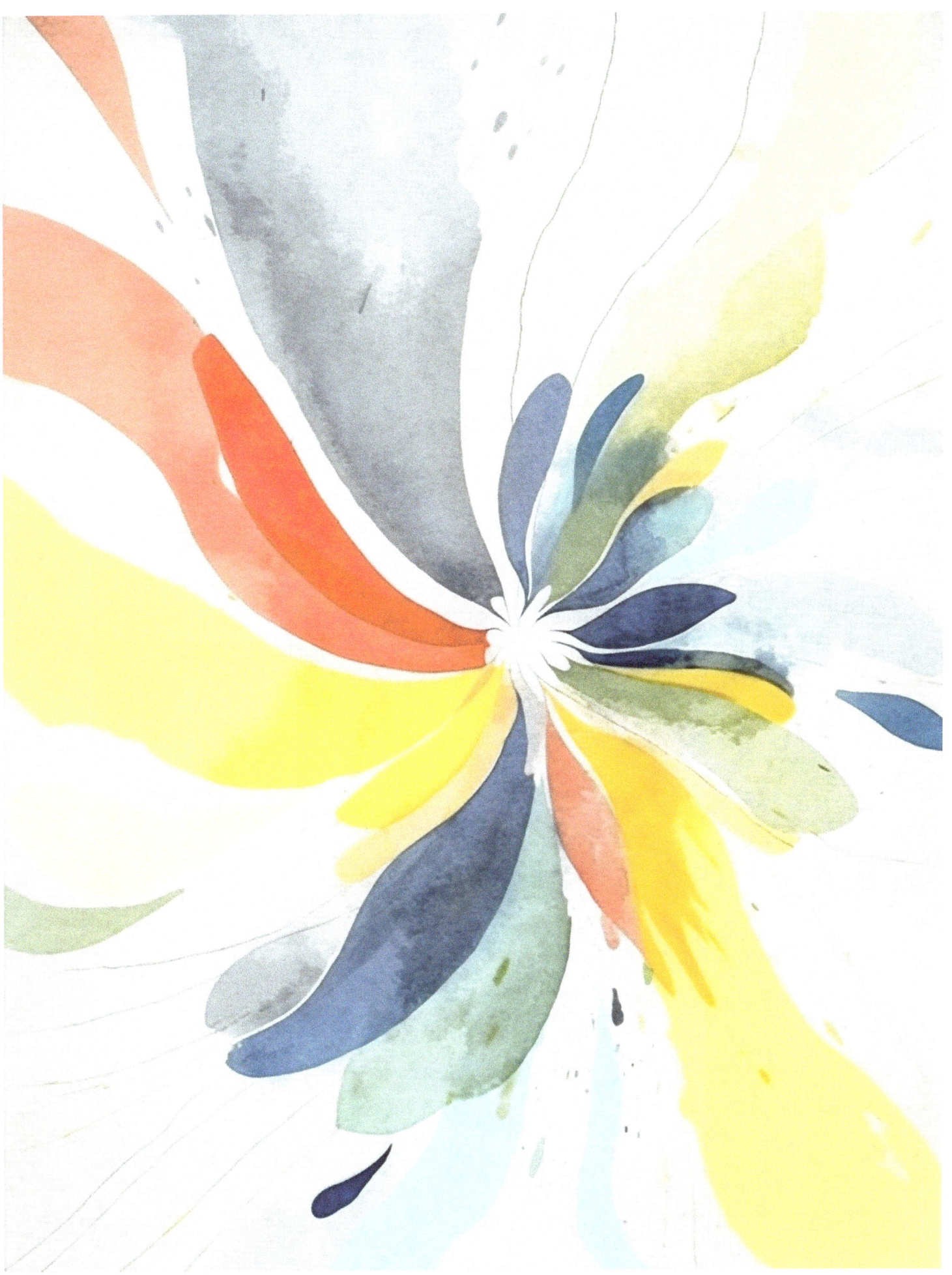

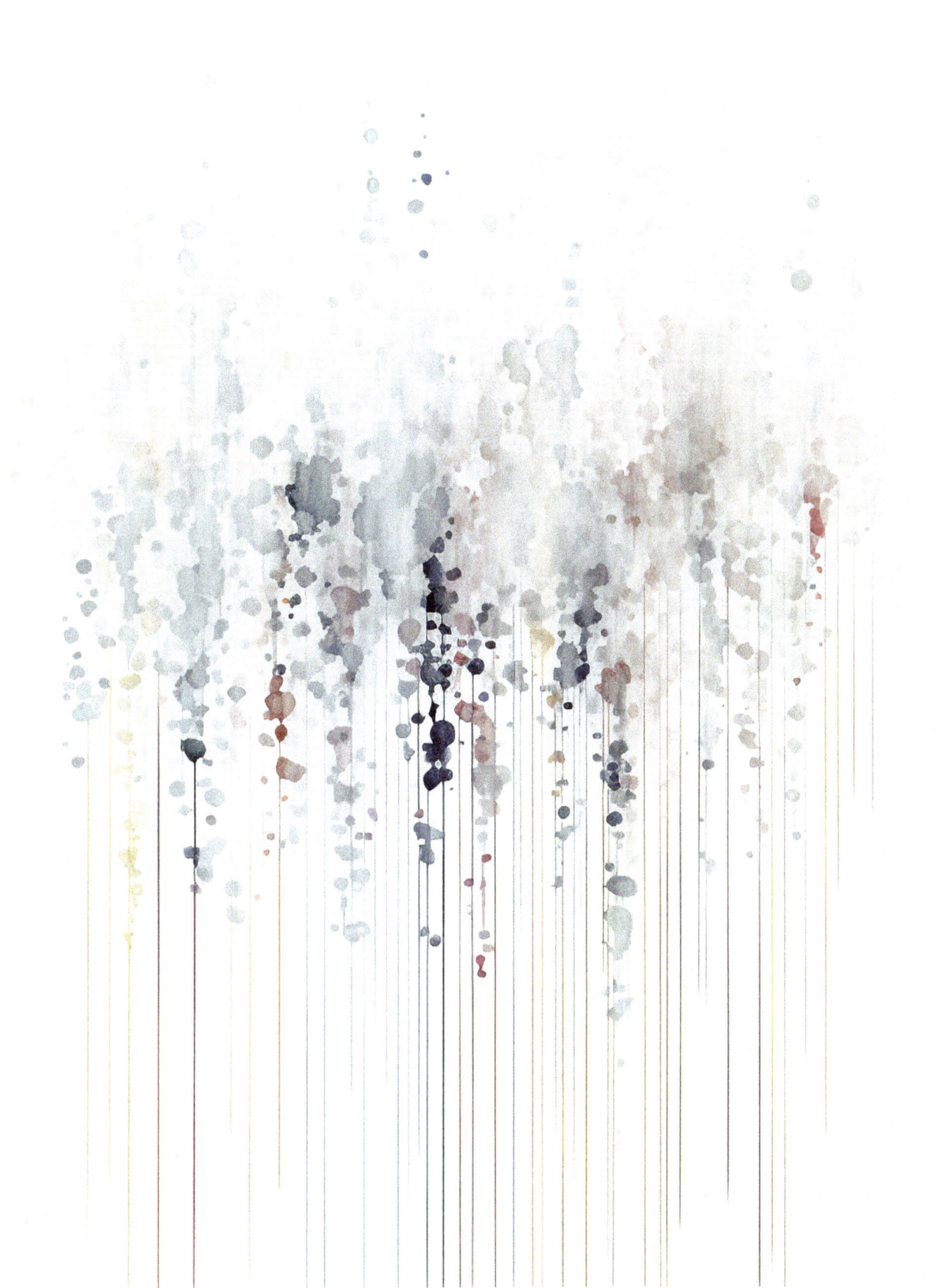

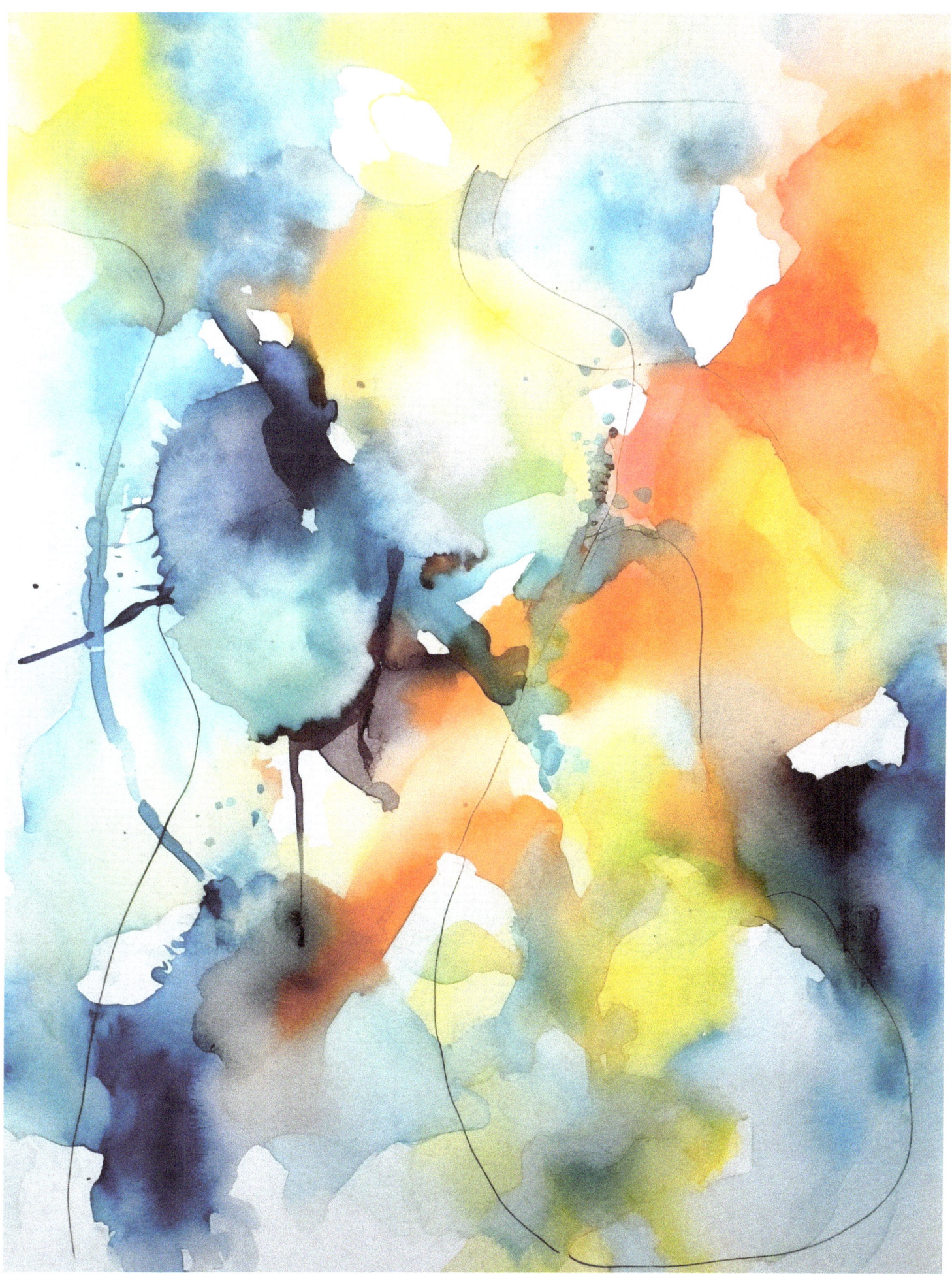

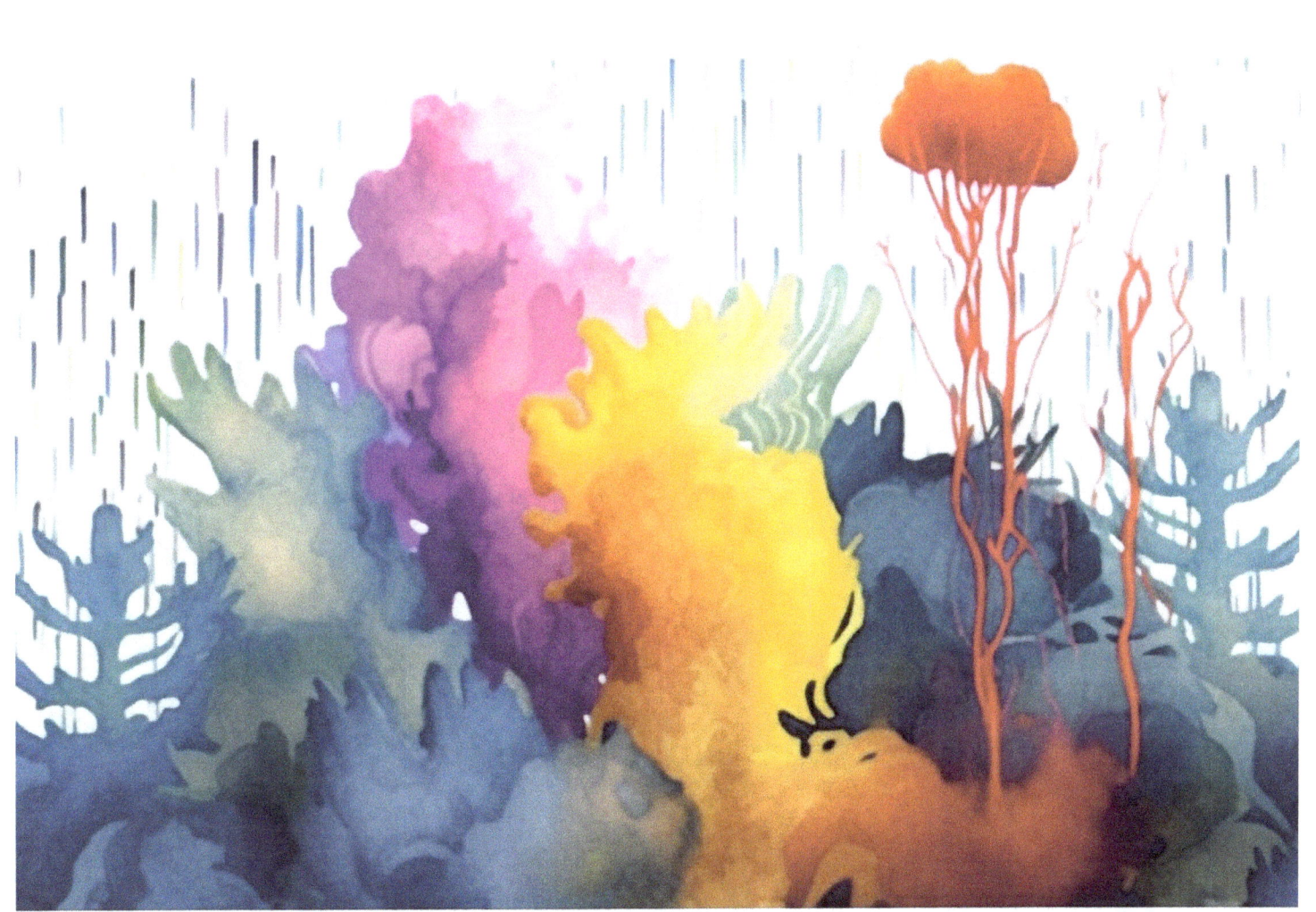

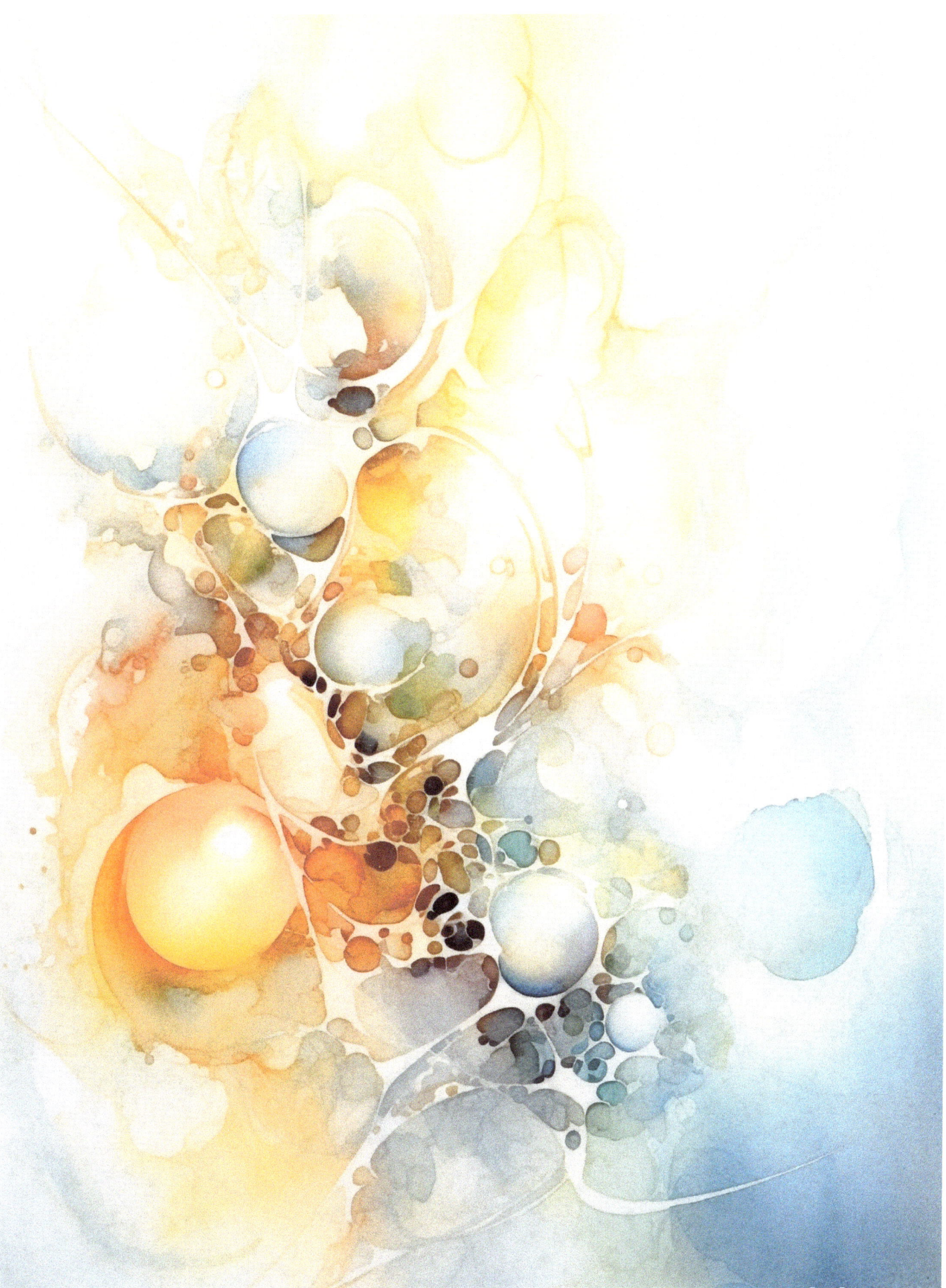

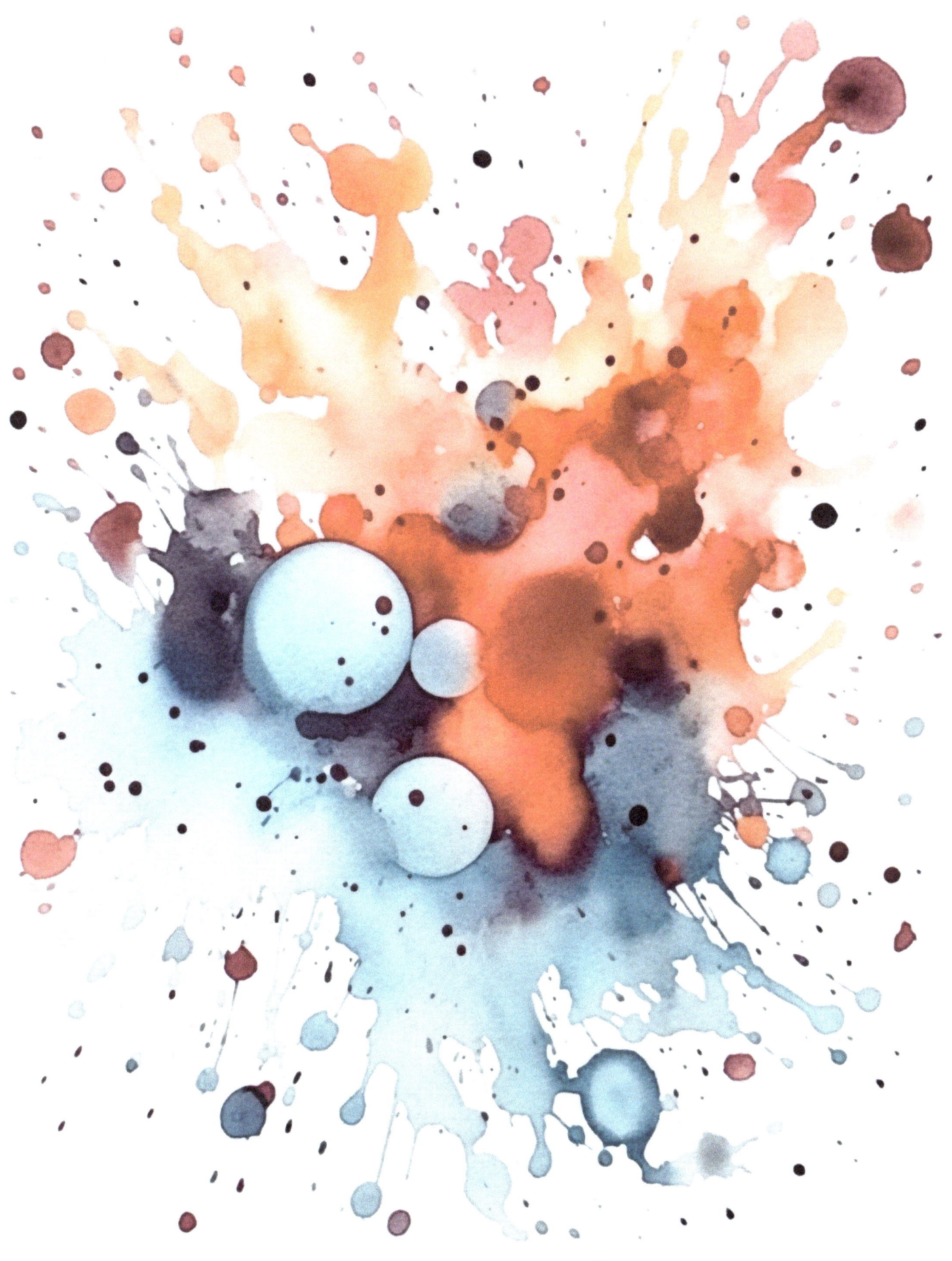

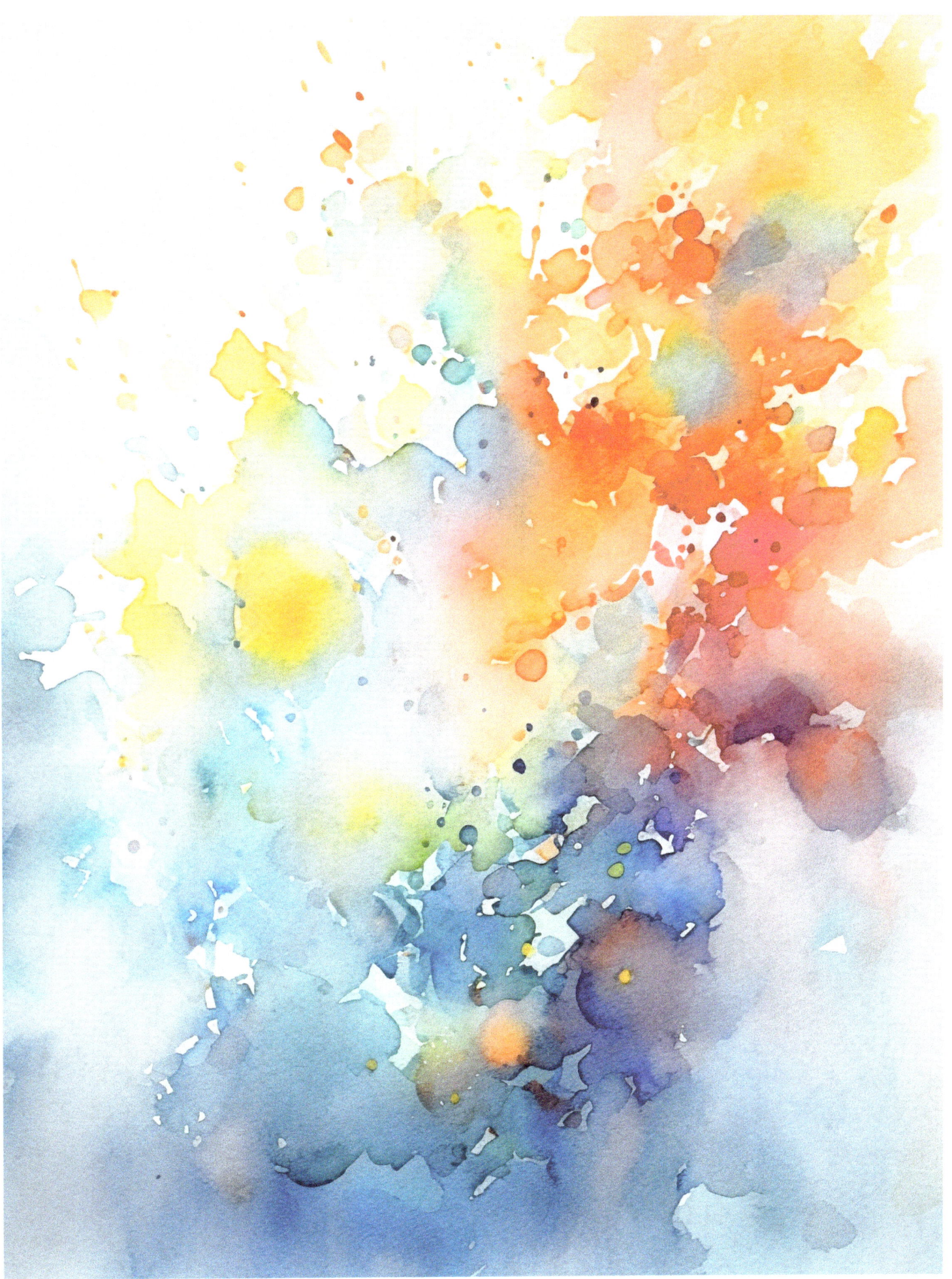

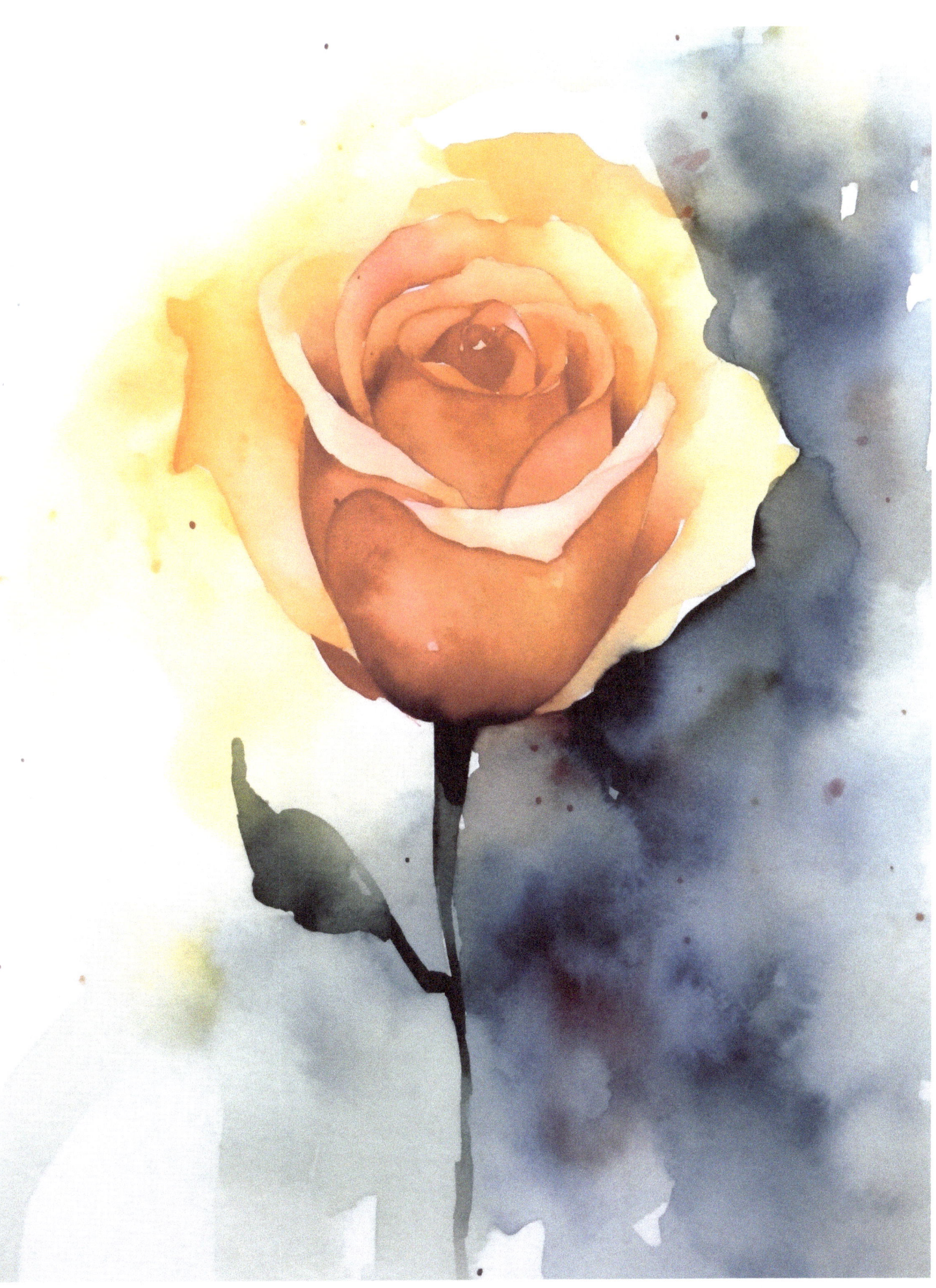

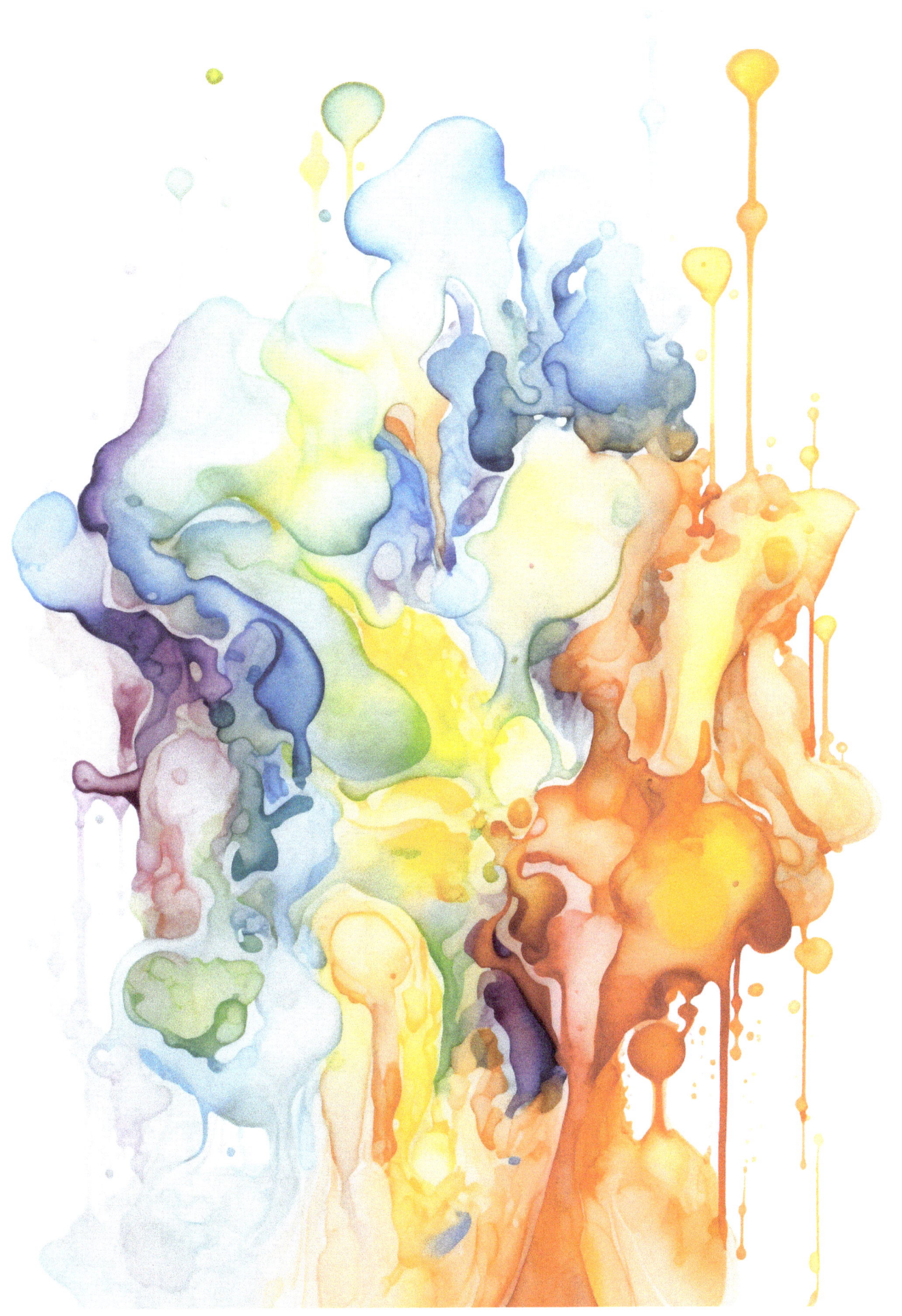

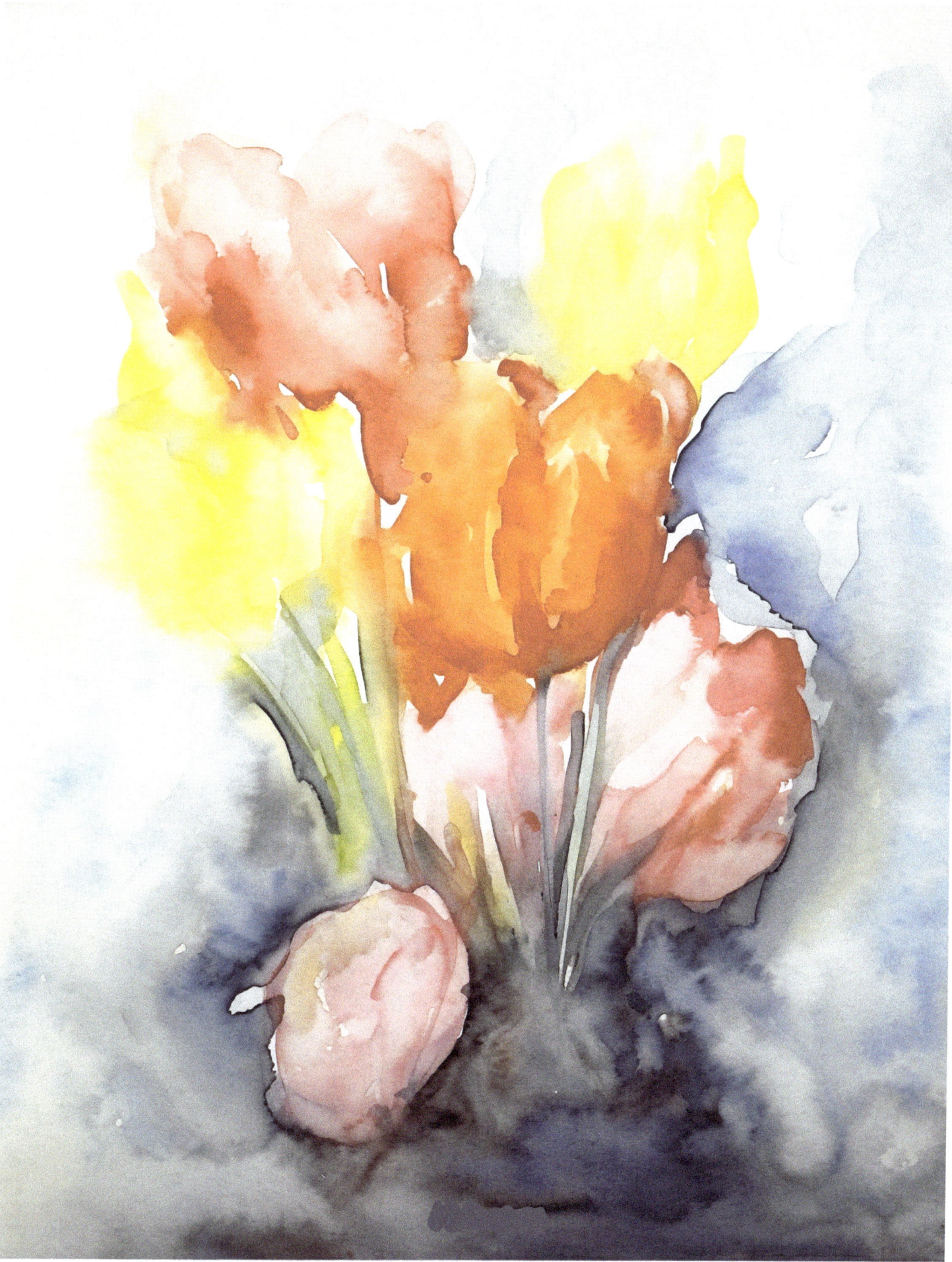

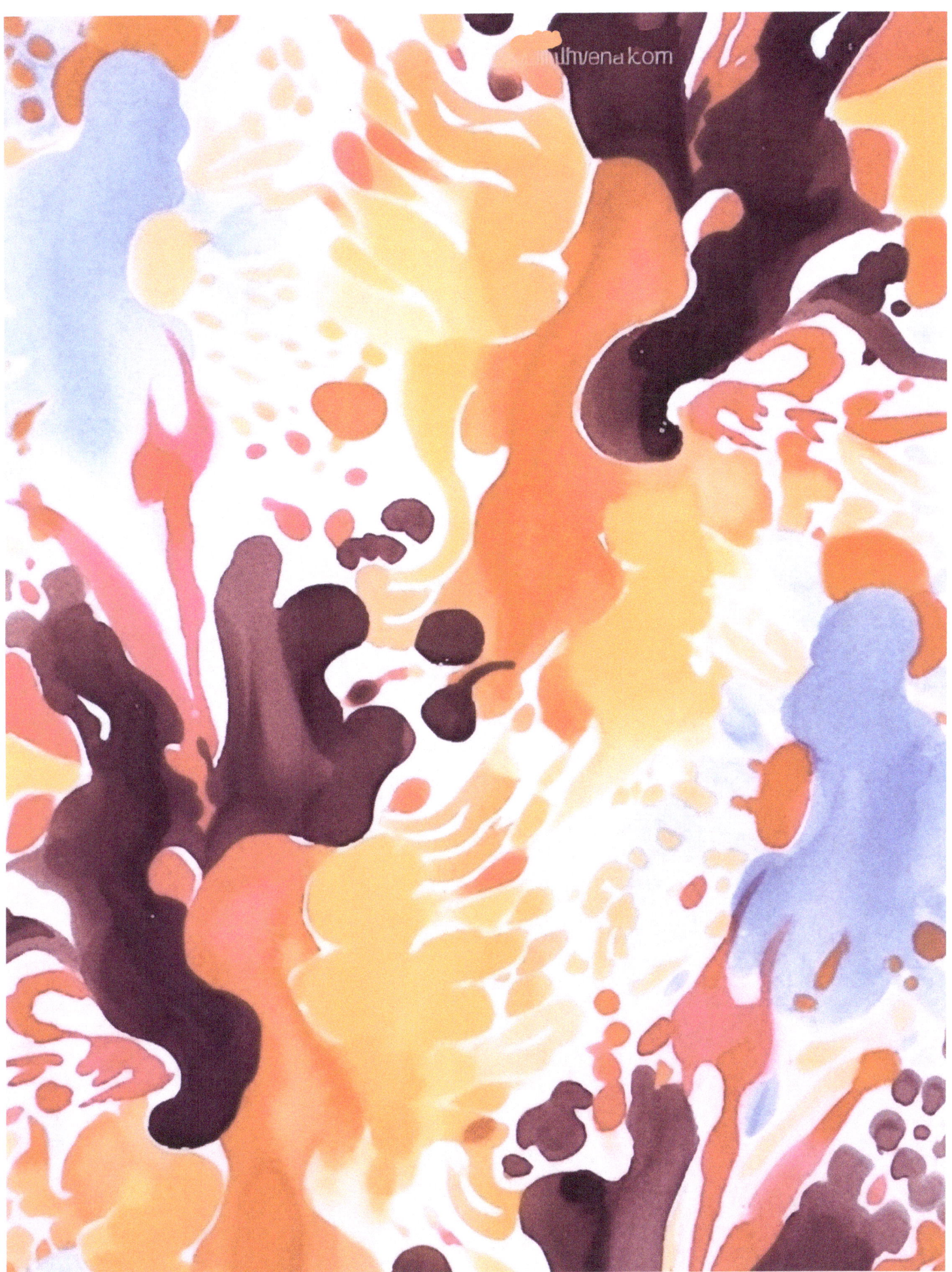

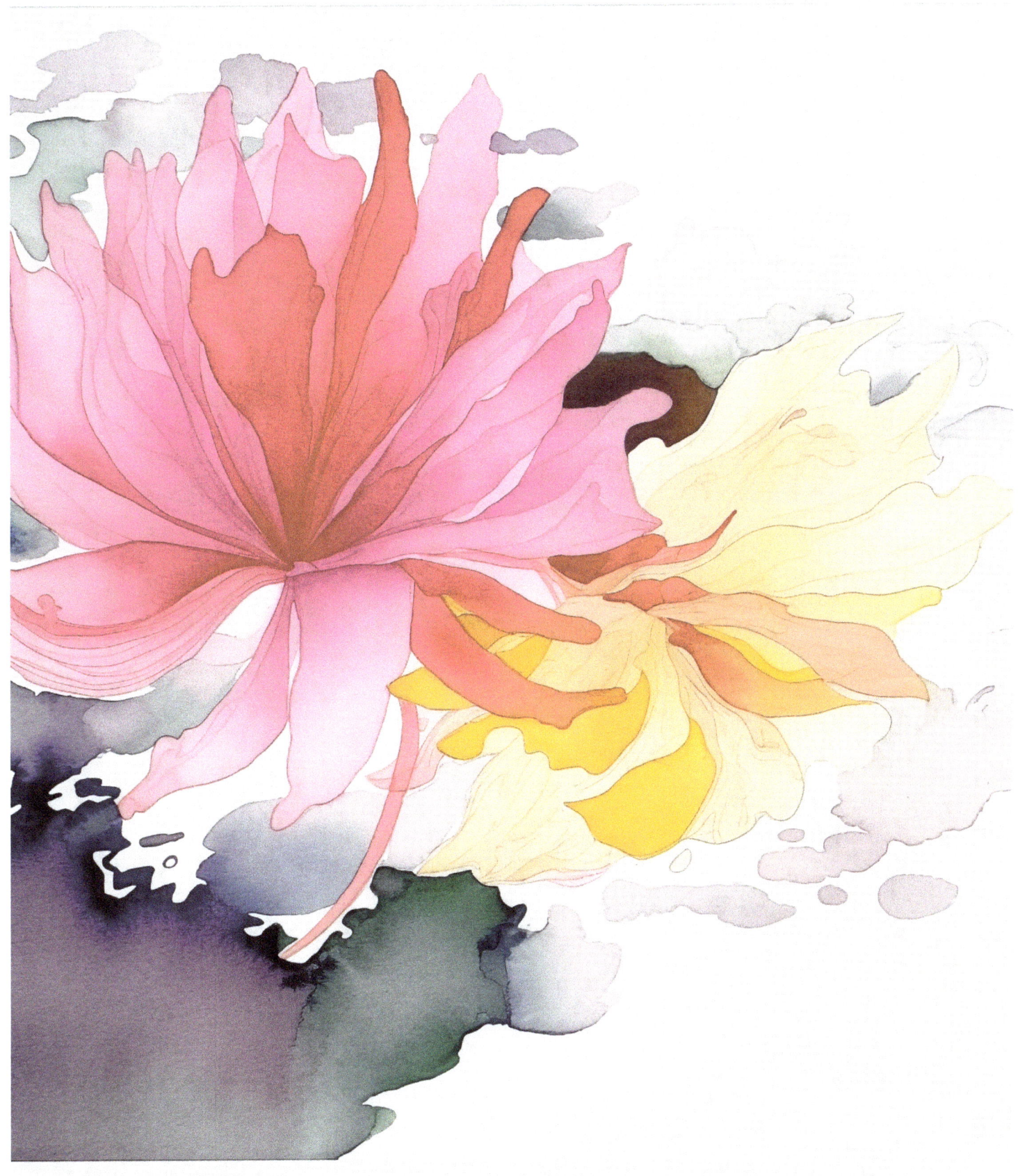

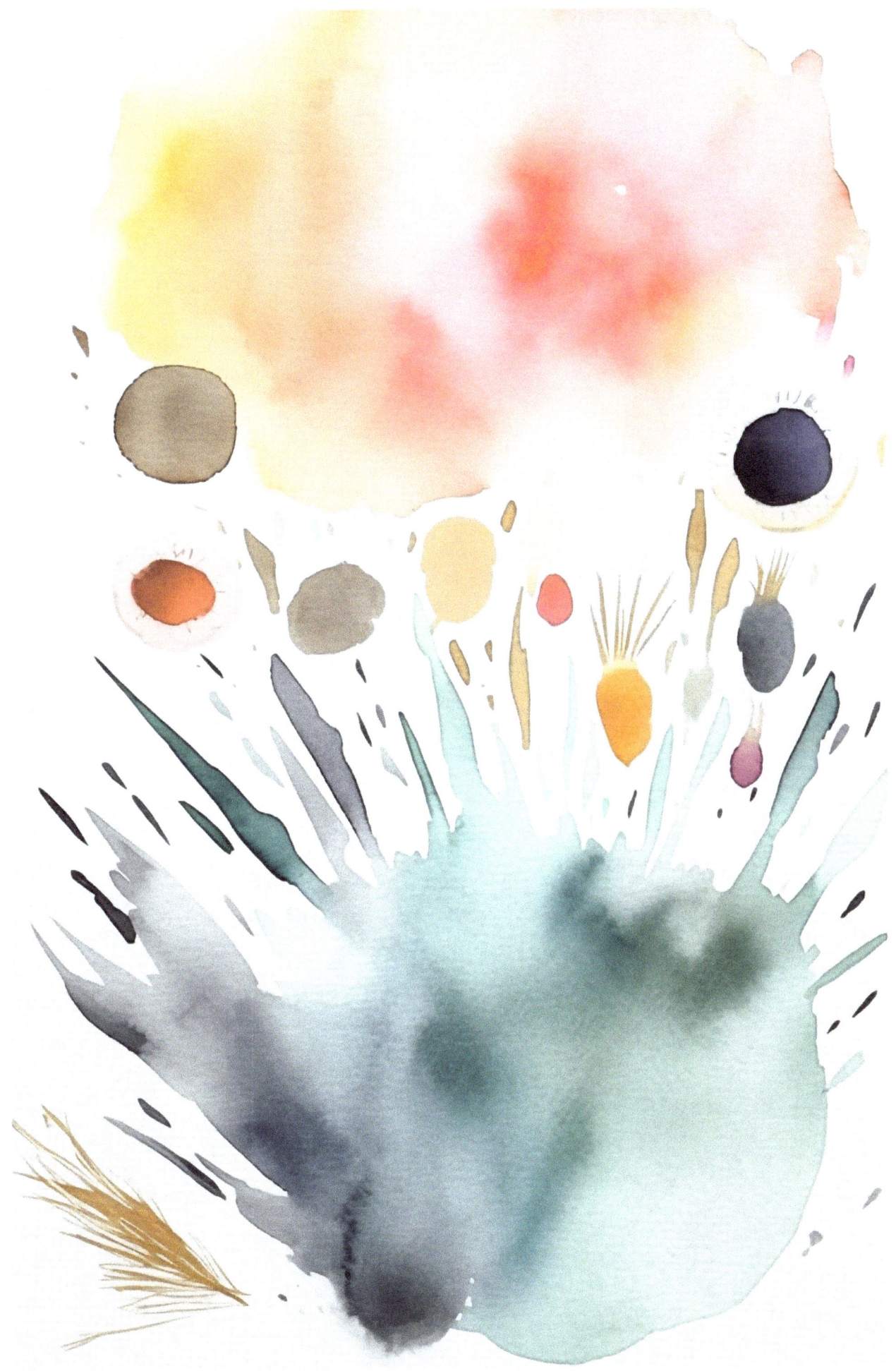

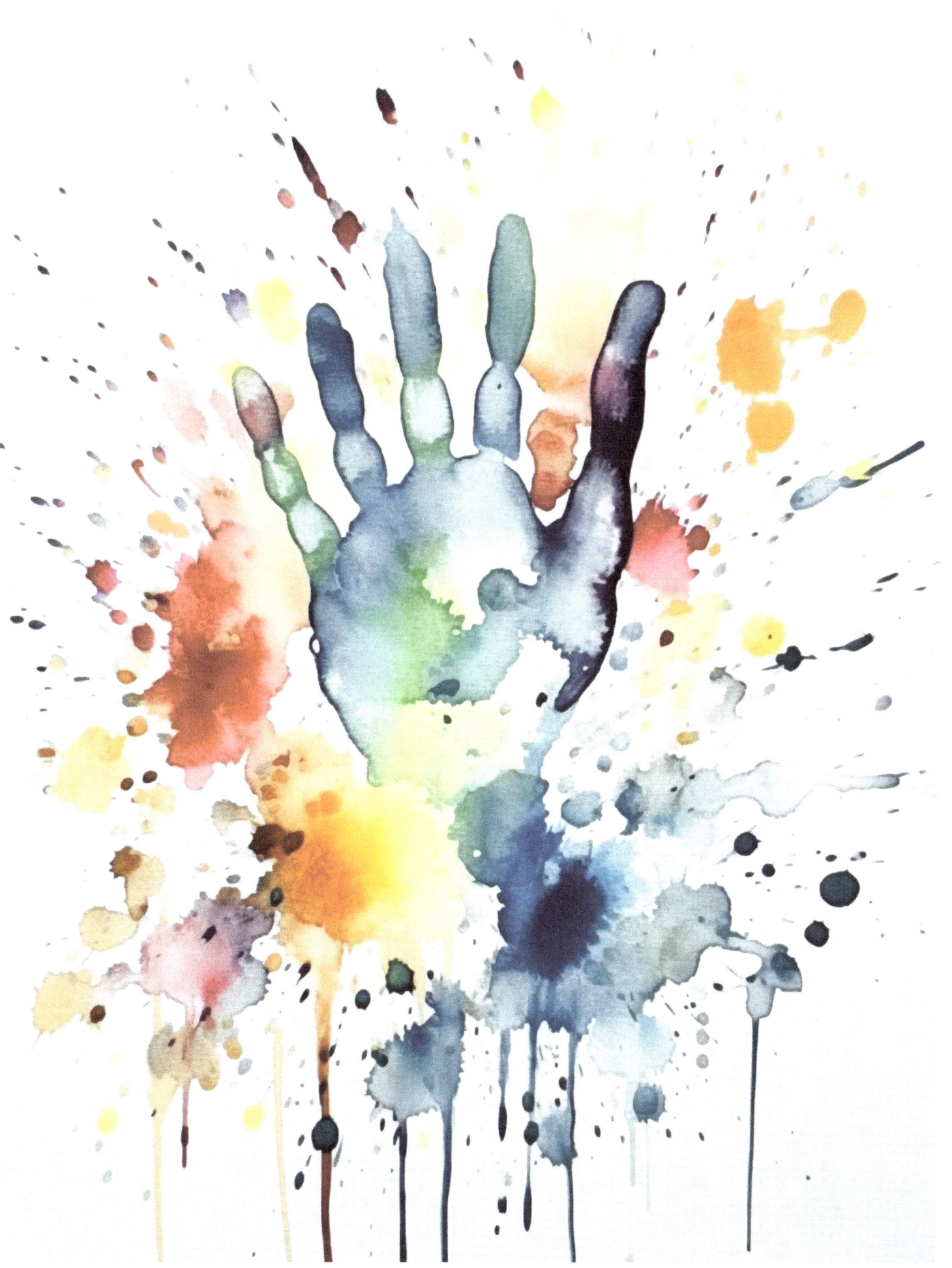